US NAVY
IN WORLD WAR II

US NAVY
IN WORLD WAR II

RONALD HEIFERMAN

CHARTWELL BOOKS INC.

A BISON BOOK

Published by Chartwell Books Inc., A
Division of Book Sales Inc., 110 Enterprise
Avenue, Secaucus, New Jersey 07094

Copyright © 1978 by Bison Books, London, England

Printed in Hong Kong

ISBN 0-89009-183-8

Library of Congress Catalog
Card Number 77-94103

CONTENTS

The carrier *Saratoga* (CV. 3) maneuvers with her destroyer escort. It is about 1933 and although biplanes still equipped US carriers, the battle-winning concept of the fast Carrier Task Force had already been tested.

Between the Wars

The United States emerged from World War I as a major power. Yet despite this fact the majority of Americans did not wish to assume the responsibilities of such power, preferring instead to return to the isolation and relative tranquility of the prewar period. Again and again the United States refused to accept her new role in world affairs, declining to participate in the League of Nations and rapidly demobilizing her military forces which had only so recently been brought up to par with those of the other powers. If it were possible, many Americans would have pulled down their 'venetian blinds' on the Atlantic and Pacific, leaving the other powers to destroy themselves in future wars. Failing this, they trusted that geographical distance and arms limitation agreements would provide the desired security. It was in this kind of environment that supporters of a strong naval posture for the United States found themselves after 1918.

At the end of the Great War President Wilson advocated a continuation of the naval construction program Congress had authorized in 1916, but circumstances mitigated against the completion of a navy 'second to none'. Debate over Wilson's diplomatic conduct at the Paris Peace Conference and the question of American participation in the League of Nations preoccupied those involved in the political arena and the question of naval arms, like many other issues, was forgotten for the moment. Ironically, however, the disposition of these major questions would have an immediate impact upon such corollary issues as military preparedness and naval arms.

Wilson's failure to involve Republicans in postwar peace deliberations turned foreign policy into a partisan issue in the United States. Overlooking the fact that Republicans had a majority in the United States Senate as a consequence of the 1918 election was to prove disastrous. Since the Constitution demanded Senate ratification of all treaties, failure to include Republican leaders in the American delegation at Paris dealt a death blow to Wilson's desire for American participation in the League and a vigorous American presence in world affairs.

Although Wilson's failure to conciliate Republican congressional leaders proved to be a blunder of the first magnitude, it was not the only reason for congressional rejection of the Treaty of Versailles and the League of Nations. There were nonpartisan considerations that contributed to the collapse of Wilson's dream not the least of which was the fact that many Americans saw the League as a threat to the national security and as a departure from their political tradition. Senator William E Borah expressed this view in November 1919 in a speech before his colleagues:

Below : The old battleship *Alabama* was used as a target for General Billy Mitchell's bombers in 1921. The ship is seen wreathed in white smoke from two 25 lb phosphorous bombs.

This treaty imperils what I conceive to be one of the underlying principles of this Republic. It is in conflict with the right of our people to govern themselves free from all restraints, legal or moral, of foreign powers. . . . Next to the tie that binds a man to his God is the tie that binds a man to his country, and all schemes, all plans, however ambitious and fascinating they seem in their proposal, but which would embarrass or entangle and impede or shackle her sovereign will, which would compromise her freedom of action, I unhesitatingly put behind me.

In expressing his opposition to the Treaty and the League, Senator Borah spoke for many of his colleagues and a sizeable portion of the American electorate. Given this situation, only a political compromise could have allowed America to ratify the Treaty of Versailles but this was not to be forthcoming thanks to the unwavering stance of the President and his critics. Thus, when the matter was taken up in the Senate in November 1919, supporters of the Treaty and the League failed to gather the necessary votes for ratification in spite of the fact that Wilson had undertaken a nation-wide speaking tour to rally public support behind his program.

Proponents of the Treaty of Versailles continued to press for Senate ratification after November 1919 undaunted by the fact that Wilson was in-

Top : The *Alabama* reels under the concussion of a 300 lb demolition bomb during the 1921 tests. Although spectacular, the Mitchell tests were not scientific and gave a misleading impression of the accuracy of aerial bombing. The ship on the left is the old battleship *Kentucky*, with her upperworks almost totally destroyed.
Above : Theodore Roosevelt, a close friend of Alfred Thayer Mahan, was the principal exponent of naval expansion at the turn of the century. As President (1901–09) he helped publicize America's 'Great White Fleet' by sending it all over the world.

The *Colorado* (BB. 45) and her two sisters were the only battleships from the massive 1916 Program to be completed. They were the first US ships armed with 16-inch guns.

capacitated by a stroke suffered during his lobbying efforts on behalf of the Treaty. They hoped that the President's illness and the mobilization of millions of Americans in support of the Treaty might provide a new climate in which some kind of compromise might be possible. Such was not to be the case. Wilson remained opposed to further concessions as did his adversaries. It remained for the American electorate to decide the issue in the election of 1920. Meanwhile, America's armed forces were being rapidly demobilized and all proposals regarding their postwar status were shelved pending the outcome of the great debate of 1920.

The 'solemn referendum' which Wilson had called for in 1920 proved to be a great disappointment to those who had hoped for a vigorous commitment to the League. James M Cox, the Democratic presidential candidate, endorsed the League in only a lukewarm fashion while his adversary Warren Harding preferred to address himself to other issues. Only Franklin Delano Roosevelt, the Democratic candidate for the vice-presidency, spoke with real conviction on this matter. With Harding's victory and the beginning of the 'return to normalcy' American participation in the League was killed and so too were the hopes of those who wished to see the US assume her role as a world power.

The Harding Administration would pursue a foreign and defense policy which depended upon international agreements on arms limitation at the cost of adequate preparedness. Indeed, even before the new administration took office, the die had been cast. By

the time Harding moved into the White House demobilization had been nearly completed. In such a milieu the efforts of the Navy Department to continue the naval construction program of 1916 fell on deaf ears. The President, the Congress and the American people were interested in cutting taxes, not in an escalation of the arms race. This frugality coupled with pacifist idealism led to a new approach to the balance of power, namely one of attempting to negotiate a multilateral agreement to curtail the arms race. The Washington Conference of 1921–22 marked a first step in this direction.

The Washington Conference was the result of several factors. In the United States congressional stalwarts such as Senator William E Borah of Idaho, feared that a continuation of the naval arms race would be an economic burden and might ultimately lead to a confrontation with Japan and/or Great Britain, who would not sit idly by while the United States Navy continued to expand. They suggested a tripartite discussion of the problem which found considerable support in Congress if not at the White House. Coincidentally the British government had also come to the conclusion that some kind of arms limitation agreement was desirable, cloaking its own fears and sensitivity in a veil of concern over a possible Japanese-American confrontation in the future. The Japanese for their part did not share the enthusiasm of some Anglo-American leaders relative to arms limitation but they went along with the call for an international conference hoping, perhaps, to use such a conference as a means of consolidating their gains in East Asia and securing naval parity with the United States and the United Kingdom.

The Washington Conference was

convened in November 1921 with a double agenda. Of primary importance was the question of naval arms limitation; second was the question of the balance of power in China and the Far East. At the opening session of the conference Secretary of State Charles Evans Hughes, the host and presiding officer of the convention, made an emotional speech in which he offered the following proposal. The United States promised to scrap all capital ships then under construction provided that similar concessions were made by the other powers. The respective navies of the major participants would then be fixed in size on a capital-ship tonnage ratio of 5:5:3 with the United States and England enjoying parity while the Japanese would be permitted to maintain a fleet roughly 3/5 the size of either of the Anglo-American allies.

Hughes' address stirred the delegates to the Washington Conference to cheers but there was little enthusiasm for his proposal at the Navy Department where the full impact of his suggestions was understood only too well. In one gesture the Secretary of State had offered to scrap at least fifteen new ships, including six cruisers and nine battleships, two of which had already been launched. Hundreds of millions of dollars in new construction were to be abandoned as a measure of goodwill by the United States. If this were not enough Hughes had also suggested that another fifteen older capital ships would be scrapped. In return Hughes called upon the British to give up 23 ships, the Japanese seventeen.

More significant, perhaps, than the number of ships the United States would scrap was the fact that those capital ships which would be left would be obsolete, since they lacked adequate protection against aerial bombs, torpedoes and mines. Although it is true that agreement with Mr Hughes' proposals would also have left the other powers with equally obsolete fleets, it is important to note that none of the other powers had committed themselves to a naval construction program equivalent to that proposed by Wilson in 1916. Undoubtedly, the United States Navy would be called upon to make the greatest sacrifice.

For the British, a moratorium on the construction of new capital ships was a blessing in disguise. The cost of World War I had been a heavy one. Once the major creditor of the Western world, Great Britain found herself on the other side of the ledger after 1918. Any continuation of the arms race would have weighed heavily on the British public. Yet pride and centuries of tradition dictated that if the Americans expanded their fleet, Britain must do likewise or lose her superiority on the high seas.

The Japanese were less enthusiastic about Mr Hughes' scheme but they ultimately accepted an 'inferior position' relative to the British and Americans in return for other concessions, the most significant of which was an Anglo-American pledge not to strengthen naval bases in Guam, Manila and Singapore. In any case the Japanese lost little in accepting the 5:5:3 ratio, since their fleet was concentrated in the Pacific as opposed to the two-ocean responsibilities of the United States Navy and the three-ocean division of the Royal Navy.

There were few difficulties in securing agreement on the 5:5:3 ratio as it applied to capital ships and to aircraft carriers but problems were encountered when attempts were made to extend the ratio to combat auxiliaries. In the end, the American delegation had to accept a treaty which did not cover

Martin T4M-1 torpedo planes armed with Mark 13 aerial torpedoes are ranged on the flight deck of the carrier *Saratoga* (CV. 3) during the early 1930s. The *Saratoga* participated in the Pacific in World War II.

A Martin T4M-1 takes off over the *Lexington* (CV. 2). The size and speed of the *Lex* and *Sara* enabled the USN to develop fast Carrier Task Forces.

this category of vessel. Strenuous objections from the British, who enjoyed a numerical superiority in small cruisers which they were not willing to sacrifice, and the French, who were eager to expand their submarine fleet, made agreement on this matter impossible. So it was left to future arms limitation discussions to resolve the issue. Since the United States Congress proved unwilling to support a vigorous program of research, development and construction of auxiliary vessels after the war, the United States Navy was to be at a disadvantage when World War II began given the fact that the other maritime powers continued to lavish money on the construction of these ships.

The Five Power Treaty limiting naval arms was signed in 1922. Although the powers agreed to scrap several ships which were under construction and certain older ones in order to achieve the 5:5:3:1.75:1.75 ratio (US:UK:Japan:France:Italy) of capital ships, concessions were made to each of the signatories. Thus, for example, in return for allowing the United States to convert two battle

cruisers into the aircraft carriers *Lexington* and *Saratoga*, the Japanese were permitted to do the same with the *Akagi* and the *Kaga*. In addition, in return for allowing the Japanese to keep the *Mutsu*, a new battleship built with 'contributions' from Japanese schoolchildren, the Americans were permitted to keep two battleships of postwar vintage, the *Colorado* and the *West Virginia*, while the British were allowed to keep one, the *Hood*.

From the point of view of those who supported the idea of a United States Navy second to none, the Washington Conference was a disaster. Of equal significance, however, was the failure of Congress to appropriate sufficient funds to bring the Navy up to treaty strength and its unwillingness to spend funds on the development of new weapons systems during the interwar period. Such restraints may have frustrated naval officers but they were quite compatible with public opinion which was much influenced by pacifist propaganda, economic developments, stubborn proponents of antiquated strategy and tactics and the lobbying of the prophets of aerial warfare.

The immediate post-World War I period witnessed a marked increase in pacifist activities of which the Washington Conference was the first concrete result. Millions sincerely believed that concessions such as those included in the Five Power Treaty represented a major step toward the preservation of world peace. If Wilson had failed to achieve American entry into the League his belief in moral diplomacy and a new more rational world order had left a deep imprint on the American people, many of whom

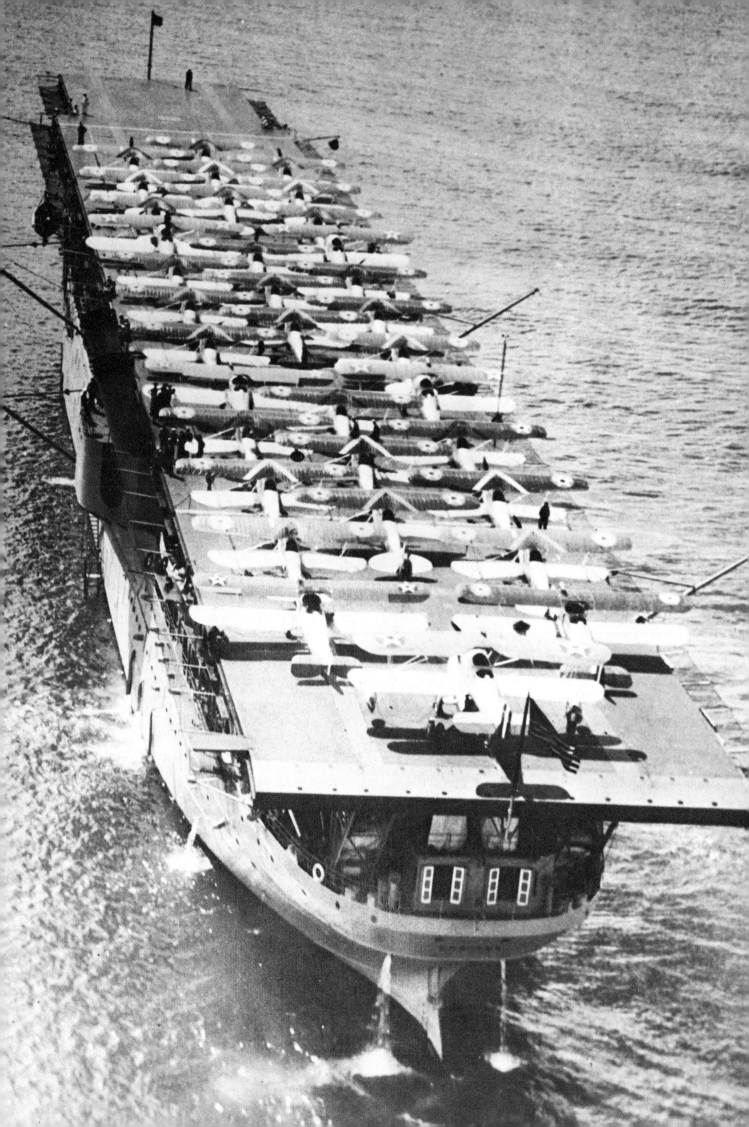

trusted that their allies and former enemies shared this vision of a brave new world. Unfortunately, events were to prove this view incorrect but, for the moment, it prevailed.

Perhaps the most outstanding result of the pacifist mentality was the Kellogg-Briand Pact of 1928 which renounced war as an instrument of national policy. Considering the relatively large numbers of signatories to this agreement, proponents of a strong American defense posture had a difficult time in persuading Congress and the American people of the need to increase defense spending. Indeed, they failed to obtain the funds necessary to bring the Navy up to treaty strength because such expenditures as might be necessary were seen as redundant in light of the Kellogg-Briand Pact. Many Americans, President Hoover included, treated the Kellogg-Briand Pact as 'a sort of incantation,' in the words of Samuel Eliot Morison, 'to preserve the peace.' More cynical newspaper reporters dubbed it 'the international kiss.'

If pacifist propaganda had been the only force mitigating against expansion of the United States Navy, it is doubtful that supporters of a large navy would have been so totally frustrated between 1920–1933. Economic developments were of equal if not greater importance in contributing to the decline of US armed forces. Demobilization following the end of World War I had a serious impact on the American economy. Millions of men returned to the labor force only to find that there was no immediate employment. When they were finally assimilated into the labor market they joined their peers in a rash of spending which triggered very serious inflation. Faced with unemployment and inflation, the Harding and Coolidge administrations looked for ways to trim government spending in order to maintain a balanced budget. Military appropriations were among the easiest targets for cost-conscious congressmen and senators. Between 1921 and 1928 Congress became increasingly niggardly with regard to expenditure on arms which might never be used. The Great Depression of 1929–1933 further reinforced this frugality.

Critics of traditional military policies provided further ammunition for those who argued against increased defense spending for economic and/or moral

reasons. Visionaries and prophets like Brigadier General William Mitchell offered alternative strategies which promised to provide adequate defense at a much reduced cost. Although it might be an exaggeration to suggest, as do some, that men like Mitchell had launched a crusade against the Navy, one cannot deny that their criticism captured the imagination of the public and challenged more traditional minds to respond, a challenge they were either unable or unwilling to take up.

For men like Mitchell the Navy, as it was constituted, was an anachronism. Except for the submarine, naval weaponry was seen as obsolete in light of the future potential of aerial warfare. According to such proponents of aerial warfare, sea power was no longer a viable first line of defense against enemy attack. Under aerial attack all surface vessels were vulnerable including the new aircraft carriers. If this vision was correct, would it not be a great waste of resources to continue to think in traditional terms?

The prophecy of General Mitchell may not have persuaded his colleagues in the Army and Navy but it captivated the public and the press. Aircraft had been of negligible importance during the Great War but aviators had acquired a mystique which defied reason and was difficult to combat. Furthermore their alternative designs promised to be more economical than the conventional weapons and they were certainly more exciting!

That critics such as Billy Mitchell were able to capture the public's attention was not entirely due to the romance or cost accounting of aircraft. One must also note the failure of the Navy Department to accept change and make an appropriate case for increased appropriations. As long as officers remained wedded to the capital ship as their chief weapon and the Battle of Jutland as their primary text, it would be difficult to overcome congressional opposition to increased spending and such revenues as were made available would be disproportionately allocated for the construction of larger ships while the development and construction of combat auxiliaries were neglected, perhaps because it was assumed that they could be quickly produced in an emergency. The fact that naval appropriations remained relatively static during the period from 1920–1933 while production costs were rapidly increasing due to persistent inflation meant that the Navy was able to purchase less and less as the years went by. Worse still, sacrifices were made in other vital research and development programs in order to channel additional funds into the large capital ship construction projects.

Despite the decline in congressional support of the Navy and the sometime mistaken priorities of the Navy Department, the reader should not be left with the impression that no progress was made during the period from 1920–1933. There were several signifi-

Three views of the Navy's first carrier, *Langley* (CV. 1). Converted in 1922 from the collier *Jupiter*, she provided invaluable experience until the completion of the *Lexington* and *Saratoga*. In 1937 the forward half of the flight deck was removed and she reverted to the status of a seaplane tender (AV. 3). She was sunk by the Japanese in February 1942.

cant developments during this period including the evolution of fleet aviation, experimentations with techniques of amphibious warfare and the development of a fleet with long-range operational potential.

Although the Army Air Corps had come to dominate aviation during and immediately after World War I, the Navy was not without an interest in aviation. Indeed, as early as 1918, naval officers pointed out the usefulness of aircraft in reconnaissance and anti-submarine warfare. In 1919 the General Board suggested that 'Aircraft must become an essential part of our fleet. A naval air service must be established, capable of accompanying and operating with the fleet in all waters of the globe.' By 1921 a Bureau of Aeronautics had been established in the Navy Department and the first seaplane tender had joined the fleet.

The Navy's development of fleet aviation was not without controversy. Critics such as Mitchell would have preferred to keep the Navy out of aviation and instigated a congressional investigation into the question of what

function, if any, aviation was to have in the Navy. In the end the Navy was permitted to keep and expand its fledgling air wing and it soon became an integral part of the service. After 1923 aircraft figured regularly in war games and in 1925 the Navy's first carrier, the *Langley*, participated in fleet exercises. Two larger carriers, the *Saratoga* and the *Lexington*, joined the fleet in 1929, by which time most senior naval officers had become enthusiastic proponents of the carrier, calling upon the Navy Department for an accelerated program of carrier development.

Of almost equal significance to the development of fleet aviation was the Navy's effort to experiment with techniques of amphibious warfare, although the size and scope of this latter effort did not begin to approximate the evolution of the Naval Air Corps. Amphibious warfare did not figure in World War I insofar as the United States Navy was concerned but it was not long after the Great War that the Marines began to experiment with amphibious concepts.

By 1933 a Fleet Marine Force had been established and shortly thereafter both the Army and the Coast Guard joined in amphibious exercises. Although the scope of American amphibious capabilities was limited, many valuable lessons had been learned during the interwar period which would be applied after Pearl Harbor.

If the development of fleet aviation and amphibious techniques were the result of conscious policy, the long-range capability of the American fleet was the result of conditions imposed on the Navy by the Five Power Treaty of 1922 and congressional stinginess, namely the lack of adequate naval bases in the Pacific. By agreeing at the Washington Conference not to expand installations in such places as Guam and the Philippine Islands, the American government forced the Navy into a position which demanded greater mobility if the fleet was to be bound permanently to Hawaiian bases.

Because the United States Navy did not have the luxury of numerous Pacific way-stations, it could not rely on a strategy linked to fixed bases separated by relatively short distances. In the construction of ships, it was imperative that they be capable of sailing long distances without refueling or being dry-docked for repair. Such repairs as were necessary had to be carried out at sea while fleet trains composed of tankers, ammunition ships and even hospital ships made it possible for the fleet to undertake extended voyages. Such independence from land bases proved to be of vital importance during World War II when mobility served the US well in the vast expanses of the Pacific.

With the election of Franklin D Roosevelt in 1932 the fortune of the Navy improved. Unlike Harding, Coolidge and Hoover, Roosevelt was an enthusiastic supporter of the Navy. Having served as Assistant Secretary of the Navy under President Wilson during World War I, FDR understood the importance of a strong naval posture as part of an adequate national defense.

Unlike his predecessors, Roosevelt believed that the United States should play a vital role in world affairs. By the

Below : The *Yorktown* (CV. 5), seen here in Hampton Roads just after completion in October 1937, was the first of a new generation of US carriers. With her sister *Enterprise* (CV. 6) she served as the model for the famous *Essex* Class of World War II, and her remarkable capacity to absorb damage at the Coral Sea and Midway Battles tipped the balance against the Japanese.

Above : President Franklin D Roosevelt and his Cabinet under the 8-inch guns of the heavy cruiser *Indianapolis* (CA. 35) at a fleet review in 1934.

time he was elected president, Roosevelt had already visited Europe more than a dozen times. Although he had not traveled in the Far East, he was very much interested in that area thanks to the influences of his maternal grandfather Delano who had been an old China hand and of the Roosevelt family's trading experience in China as far back as the eighteenth century. Few Americans had this breadth of experience and interests, nor were many prominent political leaders as internationalist in outlook as the new president.

When FDR was a young man he was much influenced by the views of his cousin Theodore and the writing of Alfred Thayer Mahan. By the time he ran for the vice-presidency in 1920 Franklin Roosevelt had combined these views with Wilsonian idealism to form the core of his 'foreign policy.' In 1920 FDR had campaigned vigorously in favor of American participation in the League of Nations and in the years between 1920–1932 he did not give up his internationalist leaning. Unlike Hoover, Roosevelt did not trust the Kellogg-Briand Pact to preserve world order. Rather, he preferred to rely upon a strong defense and American participation in international forums like the League. 'It was futile,' he often asserted, 'for Americans to imagine that they could live in smug content while the rest of the world burned in the conflagration of war.'

Roosevelt never gave up his conviction that America was destined to play an important role in world affairs and that such a role required her to have a strong Navy, but events required him to moderate these views. As a candidate for the Presidency at a time when domestic problems preoccupied most Americans, Roosevelt was forced to turn his attention to economic matters. Diplomacy took a back seat during much of his first term. This fact notwithstanding, several important decisions were made during the first New Deal which had an important impact on American defense and foreign policies later.

Shortly after his inauguration, President Roosevelt submitted the National Industrial Recovery Act to Congress. Aimed at stimulating employment opportunities the legislation included a request for appropriations for naval construction to include cruisers, destroyers, submarines and aircraft carriers. Congress had previously authorized construction of some of these vessels but had declined to provide the money to do so. Now, however, there was a more compelling reason to fund such construction since it would provide thousands of jobs.

In submitting this proposal for naval construction Roosevelt was careful to point out that building these ships would in no way violate arms limitation agreements. The 238 million dollars requested for the Navy Department's program conformed to the London Naval Treaty and was recommended by the President on that basis. In making this point perfectly clear Roosevelt hoped to disarm pacifist critics and promote congressional support for this proposal.

As originally written Roosevelt's naval construction program called for the building of some 36 ships and their naval aircraft. It was the largest program submitted to Congress since Wilson's plan of 1916 and was part of FDR's effort to bring the United States Navy up to full treaty strength. Roosevelt's proposal called for the construction of fifteen vessels in government yards with the rest to be let out to private contractors who would be required to reduce the work week of their employees from forty to 32 hours as a means of 'spreading work.' Congress approved the President's program on 16 June 1933. For the first time in years new construction began, including work on the *Brooklyn*

Class cruisers, the *Craven* Class destroyers and the carriers *Enterprise* and *Yorktown*. Progress on these projects, however, was slow because both public and private shipyards were ill-prepared to meet the new demand for their services. There was a shortage of naval architects, designers, draftsmen and skilled laborers. Nevertheless, a start had been made.

In 1934 President Roosevelt once again called for additional authorization for naval construction. In so doing he repeated his assurance that such authorization was 'to bring the Navy to the strength prescribed by the Naval Treaty entered into in 1930 and to replace ships as they became overage.' It is interesting to note that the Vinson Navy Bill, as the legislation became known, did not provide a dollar figure for construction, but rather left it up to future Congresses to fund construction as they might see fit. Roosevelt had thought in terms of constructing an additional 102 vessels over a period of years but requested and received funds for only 24 ships in 1934.

The Vinson Navy Bill was signed into law on 27 March 1934. In addition to providing funds for further naval

construction, it was also significant in that it authorized the President 'to procure the necessary aircraft for vessels and other naval purposes in numbers commensurate with a treaty Navy.' This had the effect of eliminating the limitation of one thousand naval aircraft which had been imposed by a previous statute and permitted a marked expansion of naval aviation.

The naval construction programs of 1933 and 1934 did not go unchallenged. Pacifists chided the President for spending hundreds of millions of dollars for war under the guise of defense at a time when the United States was in a more secure position than any other nation in the world. Roosevelt acknowledged this pressure at a press conference in March 1934 pointing out that pacifist groups 'did not understand' the significance of legislation like the Vinson Bill. 'The public assumes,' said the President, 'that we are going to start building those 102 ships right away. So I have to point out that this bill is nothing more than a resolution that it is still the policy of the United States to build up to the London Naval Treaty limits and having passed that resolution, it depends upon the action of future

Congresses as to whether the ships will actually be started or not.'

Although the naval construction program initiated during the first years of the New Deal represented a major step forward for the Navy, many problems remained. Manpower shortages, already a problem before 1933, became critical given the fact that Congress refused to increase the authorized maximum of 100,000 naval personnel even after providing funds for new construction. With such limits on personnel, naval vessels were often operated with less than their full complement of officers and crew. Of more critical importance was the lack of support for improvement of naval bases in the Pacific.

As new ships joined the Navy late in the 1930s the inadequacy of naval installations became acute, prompting the Secretary of the Navy to appoint an investigatory Commission in 1938 to examine this problem. Chaired by Rear Admiral A J Hepburn, this Commission made its report to Congress and the Navy Department in December 1938. The Hepburn Report called for an immediate improvement of facilities on Guam, the Philippines, Midway, Wake and the Aleutians.

Above: Captain Arthur L Bristol, Jr was the CO of the carrier *Ranger* (CV. 4) in 1934.
Below: The battleship *West Virginia* (BB. 48) fires a salute in 1934.

Congress received but did not act upon the Commission's recommendations. As a result, when the Japanese attacked in 1941 and 1942, America's position in the Western Pacific collapsed, making it impossible to protect US possessions in that area.

The *Yorktown* (CV. 5) completing at Newport News in August 1937.

Short of War

Even as President Roosevelt attempted to strengthen the armed forces of the United States, others in government sought to isolate the country and insure its neutrality in the event of another world conflict. World War I had never been 'popular' in the US and the failure of former allies and enemies to make good their war debts provided ammunition for those who had come to view the war as a cabal of international financiers assisted by the duplicity of President Wilson. Such views found increasing currency in Congress during the interwar period, ultimately resulting in the passage of legislation designed to guarantee American neutrality in the next war.

As a consequence of the efforts of the Nye Committee and other congressional isolationists such as Senator Arthur Vandenberg, the Congress of the United States passed the first of several Neutrality Acts on 31 August 1935. This statute forbade the sale of arms to combatants in any declared war and sought to prevent American flag vessels from carrying other goods to belligerents in an armed conflict. In addition, President Roosevelt was granted discretionary power to forbid Americans from traveling on belligerent vessels.

The Neutrality Act of 1935 was clearly designed to eliminate the kinds of crises that had led the US into World War I. Although such limitation of executive power was repugnant to President Roosevelt, he had little choice but to sign the measure. He dared not risk further alienation of the isolationists who had already become excited by the naval construction programs of 1933 and 1934. In signing the bill, however, Roosevelt pointed out that 'the inflexible provisions of the statute might have exactly the opposite effect from that which was intended.'

American neutrality was quickly to be put to the test as a consequence of Italy's invasion of Ethiopia in 1935 and the Spanish Civil War which commenced a year later. Shortly after Mussolini's forces invaded Ethiopia President Roosevelt invoked the Neutrality Act, but stated at the same time that although the government of the United States was determined to stay out of foreign wars one could not expect Americans to remain indifferent to assaults on freedom abroad. In the Ethiopian affair, the President believed that the invocation of the Act would hurt the Italian aggressors and called for an extension of the statute – a moral embargo – to non-military goods. In the case of the Spanish Civil War, however, the Neutrality Act worked to the detriment of the forces of freedom at a time when the fascist powers were using the conflagration in Spain as a laboratory to test new weapons, systems and techniques.

Italy's invasion of Ethiopia and the subsequent Spanish Civil War gave further fuel to congressional isolationists who sought to supplement the Neutrality Act of 1935 with yet more stringent guidelines. The Act of 1935 applied to declared wars not 'civil wars' like the one in Spain. Furthermore, the statute only restricted the sale of munitions to belligerents and not other commodities and supplies. Congressional isolationists tried to close such loopholes in 1937 when they proposed an automatic embargo on the sale and/or shipment of any goods to nations involved in wars or suffering civil strife.

President Roosevelt and the State Department lobbied hard against the concept of a total embargo, proposing in its place the so-called 'cash and carry' principle. This provided that once the President had declared the existence of a state of war in a given area, nonmilitary goods could be shipped to a belligerent state only if that government paid for such goods in cash and carried them away in ships flying a flag other than the Stars and Stripes. This compromise had the virtue of allowing the United States to aid friendly nations and natural allies while precluding American shipping from becoming the victim of blockades. Unfortunately, the 'cash and carry' proposal, which was written into the Neutrality Act of 1937, had the effect of favoring powers with

The sinking of the river gunboat *Panay* (PR. 5) by Japanese aircraft on 12 December 1937 showed that relations between the US and Japan had deteriorated almost to the breaking point.
Above : Machine gunners fire their .50 cal machine guns in a desperate attempt to deter the attackers.
Left : The *Panay* slides beneath the surface of the Yangtse.
Below : The *Panay* settles in the water before sinking after being bombed by Japanese aircraft.

large cash reserves and merchant fleets, a fact which was not to the advantage of America's friends.

The Neutrality Act of 1937 was first put to the test when Japanese forces invaded China in the summer of 1937. A clear state of war existed between China and Japan yet if he were to invoke the neutrality statutes, President Roosevelt would have deprived the Chinese of 85 million dollars' worth of licensed munitions shipments plus tens of millions of dollars of nonmilitary supplies. China had neither the cash nor merchant shipping capacity to satisfy the terms of the Neutrality Act of 1937. In light of this fact Roosevelt stretched the law and refused to declare that a state of war existed between these two powers, justifying his position by pointing out that neither China nor Japan had declared war on one another.

Roosevelt's refusal to recognize a state of war between China and Japan was a ploy designed to aid a friend and buy time. Given the restrictions imposed on the White House by Congress, it was about all that could be done but it left the President dissatisfied because he recognized that as long as the United States remained locked into an isolationist posture, it could do nothing to discourage aggression. Speaking in Chicago in the fall of 1937, Roosevelt warned Americans of the dangers of continued isolation. The President stated that international lawlessness had reached a stage where the very foundations of civilization were seriously threatened. 'Let no one imagine,' he went on, 'that Americans will escape if the epidemic of world lawlessness continues.' At the conclusion of his address, FDR suggested that democratic nations establish a 'quarantine' around the fascist powers to protect the world from further aggression.

Roosevelt's quarantine speech was designed to test public opinion but if the President imagined that his plea would result in an outcry of opinion in support of his internationalist views, he was greatly mistaken. To the contrary, the quarantine speech seemed to strengthen the hands of his critics, some of whom attempted to introduce a constitutional amendment which would deprive Congress of its right to declare war except in case of an invasion. This effort failed but Roosevelt could not ignore such powerful adversaries as Senator Nye who feared that if the President's policies were to be followed '130,000,000 people might be led into another world death march.' Fearing to antagonize them further, Roosevelt let the idea of a moral embargo die.

Although he publicly demurred from unnecessary comments on world events, Roosevelt pressed on with his efforts to strengthen America's armed forces. Events in 1938 offered little hope that fascist forces would voluntarily halt their aggression. Indeed, conditions worsened both in Asia and Europe. Given this situation it was more imperative than ever that the United States prepare for the possibility of war which loomed increasingly large on the horizon.

Congress had already authorized an expansion of America's armed forces but actual progress along these lines had been slow. In his State of the Union Address in 1938 Roosevelt declared that America's defenses were 'inadequate for purposes of national security' and asked for quick action to remedy this situation. Responding to this call, Congress passed a Naval Expansion Act in May 1938 and raised the authorized strength of all branches of the armed services. Congress refused, however, to rescind the Neutrality Acts of 1935 and 1937 which remained obstacles to a more positive policy.

If 1938 had been a bleak year, 1939 would be worse. In March 1939 Hitler's forces annexed Czechoslovakia making a mockery of the Munich Agreement. Later that month, the Spanish Republic collapsed. On 23 August Germany and Russia announced the conclusion of the infamous Molotov-Ribbentrop Pact. The following day Great Britain and Poland signed a mutual assistance agreement. By the end of August the European war of nerves had reached fever pitch.

On 1 September 1939 German forces crossed the Polish border and World War II began. Americans watched with horror as Poland was dismembered in less than one month but the United States took no steps to intervene in the crisis. On the contrary President Roosevelt issued a proclamation of neutrality on 5 September. In doing so, however, he pointed out that Americans could not be expected to remain neutral in thought and promised to press Congress for repeal of the arms embargo which prevented the US from coming to the aid of the Poles.

Above: The destroyer *Reuben James* (DD. 245) was a four-stacker veteran of World War I. She gained notoriety as the first US warship to be sunk in World War II – one month before Pearl Harbor.
Below: The destroyer *Roe* (DD. 418) was one of the new *Simms* Class built in 1937–39 to meet the Axis threat.

Isolationists feared that President Roosevelt was preparing to lead the country into the war in Europe and mounted a vigorous campaign against his proposals to modify the Neutrality Acts to permit purchase of munitions on a 'cash and carry' basis. Led by former president Hoover and Charles Lindbergh, they lobbied against any change in American policy but in the end, their policy did not prevail. On

4 November 1939 Congress passed a bill permitting the extension of the 'cash and carry' provision of the Neutrality Act of 1937 to the sale and shipment of arms, thus allowing the United States to offer some assistance to the British and the French. Ironically, neither the British nor French rushed to take advantage of the opportunity to purchase war supplies in the United States. It was not until

submarine campaign forced the British to seek additional American aid. Roosevelt and his cabinet, which now included Republicans Frank Knox as Secretary of the Navy and Henry Stimson as Secretary of War, were inclined to honor Great Britain's request but the Neutrality Acts tied their hands. Unless Congress rescinded or modified these laws, it would be impossible for the United States government or American financiers to extend credit to the British. Furthermore, American shippers could not carry such supplies as the British might need in their hour of peril. Since Britain lacked the necessary cash and surplus shipping to purchase and cart munitions and other goods, either the law would have to be changed or Britain might fall.

The plight of the British caused Roosevelt to take the initiative in

Left : Grumman F6F Hellcats en route for the UK as part of the Lend-Lease deals. The Royal Navy received 1182 Hellcats between 1941 and 1945.
Below : The new destroyer *Kearny* (DD. 432) was badly damaged by a U-Boat's torpedo during a confused convoy action off Iceland in October 1941.

the German invasions of Norway and Denmark ended the 'Phony War' that American resources were tapped.

Concurrent with his proclamation of neutrality on 5 September 1939, Roosevelt issued an executive order establishing a Neutrality Patrol. The purpose of this patrol was to track and report vessels of belligerents in the European war approaching the United States or the West Indies in order to prevent them from conducting warlike operations too close to American shores. At a meeting of the Foreign Ministers of the American Republics held in Panama later in September, the concept of the Neutrality Patrol was adopted by the other American Republics. The Act of Panama established a line beyond which belligerent vessels would not be permitted to conduct military operations but left it almost entirely up to the United States Navy to enforce this policy. Accordingly, the Navy assisted by the Coast Guard organized patrols extending from Newfoundland to Trinidad.

Between September 1939 and June 1940 the Neutrality Patrol remained the only US naval commitment related to the war. However, with the fall of France in June 1940 this situation changed. With new bases on the French coast, the Germans were in a better position to wreak havoc on shipping bound for England. They took full advantage of this situation increasing their submarine attacks to the point where shipping to and from Great Britain was being seriously

disrupted. Given its shortage of destroyers and other escort craft, the Royal Navy was unable to respond to the challenge of Doenitz's wolf packs. Accordingly, the British called upon the United States for help.

Events in Europe did not go unnoticed in the United States but public opinion still precluded an entry into the war. On the other hand, there was nothing to preclude the US from taking those measures 'short of war' which might help its friends. It was with this in mind that Roosevelt sought to bolster the British by giving them fifty World War I vintage destroyers in return for permission to establish military and naval installations in British colonies. Such a swap could be justified on the grounds that it strengthened the defense of the western hemisphere without weakening the United States.

The destroyer-naval base deal was consummated early in September 1940. As might have been expected, the German government was none too happy about the arrangement but nothing was done about it. Hitler was not yet ready to risk war with the United States, a fact which President Roosevelt realized and tried to impress upon congressional leaders. This being the case, the United States could go even further in pursuing its 'short of war' policy without risking German retaliation if events dictated further assistance to the British and indeed they did.

The mounting toll of the German

suggesting an alternative to the 'cash and carry' provisions of the Neutrality Acts. 'If a neighbor's house is on fire,' the President told a press conference in December 1940, 'you would not waste the time arguing about the cost of a hose. You would put the fire out and get the hose back afterward.' Why not apply the same principle to the UK? Give them the guns and ships necessary to win the war and worry about repayment when the war was over.

In January 1941 a Lend-Lease Bill was introduced by supporters of the administration in Congress. As drafted by the President's advisers, this bill authorized the President to sell, transfer, lend, or lease to friends such supplies as might be necessary to their defense when he deemed such transactions to be in the vital interest of the United States. The Lend-Lease program eliminated the 'cash and carry' provisions of previous statutes thus permitting the United States to facilitate the financing and shipping of much needed supplies.

After considerable debate, the Lend-Lease Act was passed in both houses of Congress and was signed by President Roosevelt on 11 March 1941. Although the Lend-Lease Act did not commit the United States to war, it marked an extension of the 'short of war' policy and immediately involved American merchant ships in the German submarine war. This being the case, the United States Navy was forced to make contingency plans to protect American merchant shipping and to participate in the protection of British-bound convoys, a responsibility which had hitherto been limited to the Royal (British) and Canadian Navies. Accordingly, it was necessary to commence joint conversations with the British and Canadian naval commands.

In reality, Anglo-American naval discussions had been initiated as early as August 1940 when Rear Admiral Robert Ghormley was dispatched to London by Admiral Harold Stark, Chief of Naval Operations, to assess the situation in the United Kingdom and enter into preliminary discussions with his British counterparts. These discussions quickly widened to include an analysis of how the United States could assist Churchill's government in its gravest hour. It was as a result of these preliminary talks that Admiral Stark became convinced that the security of the United States depended on preventing the disintegration of the British Empire. This opinion formed the basis of the Lend-Lease policy.

Founded on Admiral Ghormley's report, Admiral Stark requested authorization to enter into secret negotiations with the British to prepare a common program to be implemented when the United States entered the war. He received such authorization from Secretary Knox in November. Shortly thereafter Ghormley was instructed to contact the Admiralty in London to invite its members to send a mission to Washington early in the new year. The British readily accepted this invitation.

Joint naval staff discussions were opened in Washington on 29 January 1941 as Congress was debating the Lend-Lease Bill. The Conference had a tripartite agenda: (1) to determine the best way to defeat Germany in the event of US entry into the war (2) a

Above : The destroyer *Mayo* (DD. 422) was the second of the new *Benson* Class. In all, 96 of this Class and the similar *Livermores* were commissioned between 1940 and 1943. Her machinery is arranged on the unit system.

discussion of the mechanics of strategy and tactics in any future Anglo-American co-operative effort (3) agreement upon mutual responsibilities when war came.

After two months of negotiations an agreement was reached on 27 March 1941. Known as the A-B-C-1 Staff Agreement it provided for collaboration in planning, development of common defense policies, agreement on strategic concepts, development of clearly defined command responsibilities, exchange of intelligence and the extension of American naval protection for merchant convoys bound for England. In short the A-B-C-1 Staff Agreement provided a blueprint for a joint Anglo-American effort against the Third Reich when the United States became a belligerent.

With the conclusion of the A-B-C-1 Staff Agreement the United States Navy was committed to taking over protection of merchant convoys in the North Atlantic as soon as the Atlantic Fleet was ready to do so. This meant that American naval units had to accelerate training in convoy escort techniques, perfect antisubmarine tactics and improve communications capabilities. Fortunately, the Royal Navy was able to provide some assistance in this regard so that the United States might be able to assume its new responsibilities by the summer of 1941, the target date discussed at the Washington Conference.

In preparation for escort-of-convoy obligations, Admiral Stark created the Convoy Support Force. The Support Force was commanded by Vice-Admiral A L Bristol who was respons-

ible to Admiral King, the newly appointed Commander-in-Chief of the Atlantic Fleet. The original plan for American participation in escort-of-convoy functions called for the United States Navy to assume total responsibility for the transatlantic run but this was to prove beyond the capability of the Support Force. Accordingly, the A-B-C-1 Agreement was modified so that the Support Force would escort convoys from Argentia to Iceland from which point the Royal Navy would take over for the rest of the run to the UK.

As preparation for American participation in escort service now several weeks behind schedule continued, the situation in the Atlantic became more serious. U-Boat attacks on British shipping increased dramatically, threatening to disrupt the home front effort in Great Britain. Worse still, the Germans were preparing to extend the war to Greenland and Iceland. If this were accomplished the life line between England and North America might be seriously disrupted. Such a situation had to be avoided at all costs. Therefore, the British increased their garrison on Iceland (occupied since May 1940) while President Roosevelt moved to prepare for a possible occupation of Greenland.

On 9 April 1941 representatives of the Danish government in Washington called upon the United States to establish a protectorate over Greenland 'until such time as Denmark herself was free and able to defend the colony.' Shortly thereafter, American Naval and Coast Guard vessels began to survey the area with an eye to establishing military installations there by the end of the year.

American involvement in Greenland brought the war one step closer. In recognition of this President Roosevelt declared a State of Emergency on 27 May 1941, arguing that 'it would be suicide to wait until our enemies are in our front yard before taking measures to strengthen America.' The President's pronouncement had an immediate impact upon the Navy which was ordered to expand its coastal patrol into Caribbean and south Atlantic waters.

In June 1941 American forces replaced the British garrison in Iceland at the request of the British and Icelandic governments. The American decision to accede to this request was explained by Admiral King as a

Right : The Atlantic Charter Meeting of 10–12 August 1941: l to r – General George C Marshall, President Roosevelt, Winston Churchill, Admiral King and Admiral Stark.
Below : The *Kearny* was saved by her longitudinal framing and rugged construction.

necessary step to protect Greenland and the northern approaches to North America and to insure the continued flow of supplies from North America to the UK. Iceland remained an American defense responsibility until the end of the war but was much more an asset than a liability because of the bases established there for Allied convoy escorts.

The United States Navy did not begin its escort duty until September 1941 by which time British and American leaders had secretly met off Argentia for a further clarification of Anglo-American relations. This Atlantic Conference produced no concrete war commitment from the United States but it did help to work out the details of America's role in convoy escort: the United States Navy would assume escort duties of trans-Atlantic convoys from the Canadians at a point off Newfoundland. From this point, the US Navy would escort these convoys to a 'Momp' (Mid-Ocean Meeting Place) in the mid-

Atlantic where the British would take over while American vessels returned with a westward bound group or went to Iceland for refueling or rest. To avoid German charges that such escort missions represented a *de facto* declaration of war, the Navy maintained that American ships were only escorting supply vessels between US bases in Newfoundland and Iceland. While this rationalization represented a gross distortion of the truth, it sufficed for the moment since the Germans were still not willing to force the United States into the fray.

The inauguration of the Navy's escort service in mid-September increased the risk of German-American confrontation on the high seas. Although German submarines did not attack the first escort missions of 16 and 24 September respectively, they drew first blood on 17 October when U-Boats torpedoed and damaged the USS *Kearny*. Two weeks later, another American escorted convoy was attacked. This time an American

warship, the USS *Reuben James*, was hit and sunk. She was the first naval vessel lost to the German submarine fleet. But she would not be the last.

In November 1941 the tempo of German attacks on transatlantic convoys slowed as U-Boats were diverted from the Atlantic to the Mediterranean to support Axis efforts in North Africa but the crews of the Support Force encountered yet another foe, the brutally cold and windy winter weather of the Atlantic. For those sailors unused to the unusually heavy seas, weather-caused duress was almost more unbearable than the German attacks.

The initial confrontation between the Support Force and German U-Boats led the Atlantic Fleet Command to alter the procedures under which convoy escort groups operated. Aggressive night patrolling was ordered to ferret out enemy submarines. Zigzagging and evasive course actions were to be carried out whenever practical. Momps were to be varied,

radio silence was to be observed in transit, and captains of merchant ships were to be more adequately briefed by escort commanders. Convoys were to be routed in such a manner that patrol aircraft could be used to monitor their movement and spot enemy craft. New communication codes were to be implemented and channeled through central transmitting and reception stations in Washington and Whitehall. High Frequency Direction Finder Systems (HF/DF) were to be utilized to find and keep track of German U-Boats whose movement would be plotted at intelligence stations in England and the United States.

Even with the initiation of the measures suggested above, escort-of-convoy duty remained a hazardous chore. Given the limited number of escort craft available and their relatively antique vintage, the Support Force operated under severe handicaps which would not be alleviated until newer vessels joined the fleet. For the moment, however, the Support Force

had to make do with what it had and thanks to the efforts and improvisations of the men involved in the escort service, the life-line between North America and Britain was kept open. The 'short of war' policy of the United States had achieved its end. The United States soon became an active belligerent.

Top right: Secretary of the Navy, Frank Knox confers with General Mark Clark of the 5th Army and Vice-Admiral Kent R Hewitt in the Italian Theater, October 1943.
Right: The Commander in Chief Pacific Fleet Admiral Husband E Kimmel confers with his staff in 1941. Kimmel was in command at the time of the Pearl Harbor attack.
Below: A typical destroyer of the prewar period, *Rhind* (DD. 404) of the *Benham* Class, was launched in 1938.

Pearl Harbor, 30 October 1941, just as tempting a target as it would appear to Japanese pilots five weeks later.

Day of Infamy

Although the American 'short of war' policy was based on the axiom that the greatest danger to the United States was posed by Hitler's Third Reich, Americans were also keenly aware of the deteriorating situation in East Asia. The Manchurian Incident of 1931 and Japan's subsequent invasion of China proper in 1937 had strained Japanese-American relations (none too close since World War I) almost to breaking point and some suggested that if war came to the United States it would very likely be the result of a Japanese and not a German attack. While this position represented a minority opinion, it could not be dismissed out of hand. Indeed, with a colony in the Philippine Islands, the United States was a Pacific power with a vested interest in the preservation of the *status quo* in the area. As such, American policies were often at odds with those of the Imperial Japanese government.

America's position in the Pacific dictated that the Navy play an increasingly important role in that sea and soon after the end of World War I, a major part of the United States Fleet was dispatched to permanent stations in the Pacific to supplement the Asiatic Fleet which patrolled China's coast

Above : Zeros warm up, ready to take off from the flight deck of the carrier *Kaga* for the attack of Pearl Harbor.
Right : An Aichi D3A 'Val' dive-bomber wheels over Pearl Harbor on the attack, 7 December 1941.
Below : The flight deck crew of the carrier *Kaga* cheer in the early light of dawn as a Nakajima B5N 'Kate' torpedo bomber takes off for Pearl Harbor.

and inland waterways, occasionally returning to the Philippines for infrequent visits. After 1922, the United States maintained two fleets in the Pacific, the Pacific Fleet with its home base in Hawaii and the Asiatic Fleet with headquarters in Manila and Shanghai. This fact notwithstanding, during the interwar period American naval power in the Pacific declined in comparison to Japan's strength as a consequence of US adherence to the naval arms limitation agreements even after the Japanese had announced their intention to renounce such agreements and increase the size of their fleet.

As storm clouds darkened over Asia following the China Incident, the Navy was forced to re-evaluate its position in the Pacific and develop new contingency plans. In May 1938 Rear Admiral Thomas Hepburn was commissioned to investigate America's naval defenses and report back to the Secretary of the Navy and Congress

at his earliest convenience. His findings were presented to Secretary Knox on 1 December 1938 and quickly became the focus of considerable discussion.

In sum, Hepburn suggested that America's defenses in the Pacific were grossly inadequate and suggested the following remedies: (1) reconnaissance stations and submarine bases should be established in Alaska (2) naval air stations should be expanded in the Hawaiian Islands (3) Midway and Wake Islands should be developed as patrol stations with capabilities of serving as refueling depots (4) Guam should be developed as an advanced fleet base with adequate air cover. Congress eventually acted upon the first three recommendations of the Hepburn Commission but Guam was not developed as a forward base for fear that doing so might be viewed as a provocative act by the Japanese government.

As Congress considered the Hepburn Report, the war in China continued and in the process, American ships and shore installations suffered continual harassment. At the time of the Panay Incident in December 1937, American public opinion was satisfied with an apology from the Japanese but by 1939, such apologies no longer sufficed. Accordingly, the Roosevelt administration began seriously to consider applying economic sanctions

Left: An enormous column of spray from a torpedo-hit on the *West Virginia* (BB. 48) towers over Battleship Row at 0800 on 7 December.
Below left: A more distant view of Ford Island and Battleship Row.
Below: The magazine of the destroyer *Shaw* (DD. 373) explodes, silhouetting the forward guns of a battleship. The *Shaw* was rebuilt and returned to service.

against Japan if the war in China was not brought to a halt. Since the Japanese-American Treaty of Commerce was due to lapse in 1940, the time was ripe for a discussion of such sanctions.

After considerable debate, the Roosevelt administration decided not to renew the Japanese-American Treaty of Commerce and thus opened the door to the possibility of imposing sanctions. Soon thereafter, a system of licenses for exports destined for Japan was inaugurated. While no immediate steps were taken to limit Japanese-American trade, the vehicle for imposing such an embargo in the future was now in place. Given the fact that American firms supplied the Japanese with a large percentage of their imports of many vital raw materials, it was hoped that the Japanese government would reassess its foreign policy in the light of the new license system.

Although Japanese leaders were eager to avoid a confrontation with the United States, they were unwilling to retreat from China. On the contrary, the Japanese had expanded their concept of a New Order in East Asia to include all of Southeast Asia. As originally proposed by the Japanese government in 1938, the New Order would link Japan, Korea, China and Manchuria in an economic and political commonwealth. By 1940 this pan-Asian ideal had been expanded to include the Southeast Asian colonies of the European powers in what was called the Greater East Asia Co-Prosperity Sphere.

The Co-Prosperity Sphere was even more attractive than the previous call for a New Order because of the economic potential of this larger new unit and the relative ease with which these Southeast Asian colonies might be added to the Japanese empire. Had it not been for the fact that the United States would certainly object to such a move and implement economic sanctions, the Greater East Asia Co-Prosperity Sphere might have become a reality in 1940. For the moment, however, the Japanese were not willing to risk such a confrontation.

Stalemated in China and frustrated by America's refusal to recognize her vital interests in the Far East, Japan's leaders turned to the Axis powers for support in their efforts to establish a Greater East Asia Co-Prosperity Sphere. In 1936 Japan and Germany had signed an Anti-Comintern Pact but this agreement did not define Japan's 'rights' in East Asia. What the Japanese leaders really desired was an agreement with Hitler, whose armies now occupied most of Western Europe, which would give them the green light to expand into Southeast Asia.

Above: Oil slicks spread ominously at Pearl Harbor. The white patches at the extremities of the battleships are awnings, spread to offer shade.

Under the watchful eye of Foreign Minister Yosuke Matsuoka, Japanese-German negotiations proceeded rapidly, culminating in the signing of the Tripartite Pact with Germany and Italy on 27 September 1940. The signatories of this agreement sought to insure Hitler's New Order in Europe and Japan's Co-Prosperity Sphere by providing for a two-ocean confrontation should the United States seek to challenge Japan or Germany. In Berlin and Tokyo it was hoped that the threat of such a two-front confrontation would neutralize American power.

The signing of the Tripartite Pact increased the likelihood of a Japanese-American confrontation and led the governments of the United States and Great Britain to consider what joint action they might take in the event of war with Japan. Conversations of a similar nature relative to the situation in Europe were already under way and it was only natural that they be extended to include a discussion of the balance of power in the Pacific. With war looming on the horizon, casual conversation between the US and British navies no longer sufficed. Accordingly, at staff discussions in London in late 1940 and in Washington early in 1941, the situation in the Far East became a major item on the agenda.

As Anglo-American staff discussions were to prove, American and British views of the situation in the Pacific differed significantly. The British were primarily concerned with the defense of Singapore which they believed was vital to the defense of the Malay barrier in the event of war with Japan.

The Americans, on the other hand, believed that Singapore could not be defended in case of war. They refused to commit the Pacific Fleet for the purpose of reinforcing that port for fear that to do so would be to fragment and weaken America's already inadequate forces in the area. Discussions in London were concluded without breaking that stalemate.

At the A-B-C-1 Staff Conference in Washington, the question of war with Japan was discussed within the broader context of global strategy. It was agreed that the US and UK should attempt to avoid war with Japan but that if such a conflict came to pass, the war in Europe would be given first priority status while the Anglo-American allies employed a policy of strategic defense against Japan. The stalemate over Singapore was resolved by an agreement which (a) stated that the role of the Pacific Fleet was to support the defense of the Malay barrier by diverting enemy strength by attacking the Marshall Islands and (b) granted the United States Navy exclusive jurisdiction over the security of the Hawaiian Islands, the Panama Canal and the Pacific coast of North and South America.

An uneasy peace prevailed in the Pacific until the summer of 1941 when Japanese forces occupied southern Indo-China. This alteration of the *status quo* led President Roosevelt to freeze all Japanese assets in the United States bringing Japanese-American commerce to a halt. This action convinced Japanese leaders that the United States would no longer sit idly by, while Japan expanded to the south. Although war appeared increasingly inevitable in Tokyo, a last effort was made to resolve Japanese-American differences through diplomacy.

Admiral Kochisaburo Nomura, Japan's new Ambassador to the United States, was well known for his 'pro-American' views and his dispatch to Washington was designed to assure the Roosevelt administration that the Imperial Japanese government desired a peaceful resolution of the situation in Asia. Before leaving for the United States, Admiral Nomura was instructed to initiate a dialogue with Secretary of State Cordell Hull to inform him that Japan was ready to renounce further use of force in Asia if the United States moved to restore normal economic relations with Japan and served as an intermediary in arranging peace talks with Chiang Kai-shek.

Hull's response to Nomura's proposal was less than enthusiastic. He suggested that before Japanese-American trade relations could be normalized, the Japanese government would have to recognize several basic axioms including: (1) respect for the territorial integrity and sovereignty of all states in Asia (2) non-interference in the internal affairs of any Asian state (3) acceptance of the principle of the Open Door (4) renunciation of the use of force to achieve economic and/or political ends.

Hull's reply to Nomura could not have been acceptable to Japan. Hull's preconditions represented a renunciation of all Japanese activities since 1931. No government could survive in Tokyo if it accepted such terms. On the other hand, the Japanese were not ready to give up the idea of a diplomatic settlement with the United States. Thus, Japanese-American negotiations continued into the summer of 1941. At the same time, plans for war with the US were also being discussed.

In considering the alternative of war with the United States, two factors were of primary concern to the Japanese government: weather conditions and Japan's stockpiles of vital commodities. Given the limitation of resources at their disposal, the Japanese could not endure a long war nor could they expect a total victory over the United States. What was called for was a limited pre-emptive strike designed to neutralize the Pacific Fleet at Pearl Harbor while Japanese forces simultaneously invaded Burma, the Dutch East Indies, Malaya and the Philippines. Once the Greater East Asia Co-Prosperity Sphere existed, it was hoped that a diplomatic settlement

could be reached with the Western powers.

If economic factors dictated a limited strike against the United States, weather conditions necessitated that such action be taken before the middle of December 1941. This fact was reported to the Supreme War Council in Tokyo on 6 September 1941 at which time preliminary plans for the simultaneous attacks on Pearl Harbor and other targets in Southeast Asia were presented and approved. War games began off the Japanese coast later that month.

As preparations for war commenced, Prime Minister Konoye was forced to resign and was replaced by General Hideki Tojo on 18 October 1941. Tojo's elevation to Prime Minister eliminated what little influence non-military leaders exercised within the government and facilitated the effort to mobilize the country for war with the United States. While such mobiliztion proceeded, one last effort at diplomacy was tried: the Kurusu Mission was dispatched to the United States.

The Kurusu Mission had little chance of success since the Tojo government was unwilling to make any concessions beyond those originally offered by Admiral Nomura a few months earlier but it served to delay the breakdown of negotiations by several weeks, giving both sides more time to prepare for a possible military confrontation. Efforts had already been taken to bolster American Pacific defenses but time was needed to complete such preparations. Hence, Secretary of State Hull was instructed

to postpone rejection of Kurusu's proposal as long as possible.

By the end of November it was clear that the diplomatic situation was hopeless. Accordingly, on 24 November Admirals Hart and Kimmel were warned to expect an enemy attack but the place and timing of such an attack were left unspecified. About the best Admiral Stark could suggest was that it appeared likely that the Japanese would strike Guam or the Philippines. The possibility of an attack on Pearl Harbor was not even considered.

On 26 November Secretary of State Hull rejected Ambassador Kurusu's call for American recognition of the *status quo* in Asia and once again reiterated the position of the United States that Japan must evacuate China and Indo-China before economic relations could be stabilized. Although Kurusu and Nomura dutifully cabled the text of Hull's note to Tokyo, for all purposes, meaningful negotiations between Japan and the United States had ground to a halt. The next day, Admiral Stark sent the following alert to Hart and Kimmel:

This dispatch is to be considered a war warning. Negotiations with Japan looking towards stabilization of conditions in the Pacific have ceased. An aggressive move by Japan is expected within the next few days. . . . Execute appropriate defensive deployment. . . .

The Navy War Plan, adopted at the A-B-C-1 Staff Conference in March 1941, considered the possibility of a Japanese attack on Pearl Harbor but

few senior officers thought such a raid to be a realistic possibility. Admiral Stark's alert of 27 November ignored the possibility that Pearl Harbor might be the focus of Japan's attack and suggested, instead, that the Philippines, Thailand or Borneo were the most likely Japanese targets. As a result of such thinking, Kimmel took only minimal precautions against an attack at Pearl Harbor, reflecting the view of the majority of his colleagues that 'the Japs would never sail into us.'

Unknown to Stark, Kimmel and Hart, Japan's Pearl Harbor armada had put out to sea even before the breakdown of negotiations on 26 November. Consisting of six carriers, two battleships, three cruisers and dozens of smaller vessels, the Japanese attack force steamed toward Pearl Harbor over its circuitous course unnoticed by American intelligence. In planning what route was to be taken to Hawaii the Imperial Navy had consciously avoided using sea lanes normally traversed by merchant shipping. Furthermore, they avoided having the attack group pass near any American naval air stations from which spotter planes might safely operate. Although such a routing called for the passage of the Japanese fleet through heavy seas and foul weather, it moved towards its target without being detected, arriving off the coast of Oahu on the evening of 6 December 1941.

The Japanese fleet reached its attack position some 275 miles north of Pearl Harbor the next morning, 7 December, at 0600. At 0700 the first wave of attack planes were sent aloft

Right: The old light cruiser *Raleigh* (CL. 7) lists to port while being pumped out after Pearl Harbor. She returned to duty in mid-1942.

and on their way to Pearl Harbor where American forces were still recovering from shore leave and the liberties of the night before. Except for the absence of the fleet's four carriers, the entire Pacific Fleet was in port when the first wave of Japanese planes passed overhead.

Thanks to local intelligence operatives in Hawaii, the Japanese knew the precise position of their victims and wasted little time completing their mission. Of the more than ninety ships of the fleet based at Pearl Harbor, the eight battleships were their first target. Between 0800 and 0830 Japanese planes concentrated their attack on these dreadnoughts moored off Ford Island. Although an alert was sounded at 0758 – AIR RAID, PEARL HARBOR, THIS IS NO DRILL – little could be done to protect the backbone of the Pacific Fleet. By 0845 two of the battlewagons had been sunk and another five had been seriously damaged. Only the *Nevada* managed to break clear and move away from her mooring place but she too was seriously damaged by Japanese dive bombers later in the morning.

Shortly after the first wave hit Pearl Harbor, another attack group zeroed in on Army and Navy air stations at Kaneohe Bay, Ewa, and Wheeler and Hickam Fields. The damage inflicted during these raids was almost equal to the destruction of the battleships off Ford Island. Aircraft parked wing to wing made easy targets. By 1000 the Japanese had successfully neutralized American air power in Hawaii.

At midday the Japanese task force retreated, leaving American officials to tally the damage resulting from the surprise attack. The toll was horrendous. In less than 120 minutes the Pacific Fleet had been destroyed with a loss of over two thousand men. The battleships *Arizona* and *Oklahoma* lay at the bottom of Pearl Harbor while the other six battleships of the fleet, *California*, *Maryland*, *Nevada*, *Pennsylvania*, *Tennessee*, and *West Virginia*, had been seriously damaged. The Japanese attack was a tactical success. The United States had been forced into war.

Left: A wrecked B-17 at Bellows Field, one of hundreds of Navy and Army planes destroyed during the Japanese raid on Pearl Harbor.
Right: The towering pillar of smoke marks the end of the battleship *Arizona* (BB. 39) after a bomb penetrated her forward magazine. Her rusting hull still contains the bodies of hundreds of crewmen and is preserved as a war memorial.

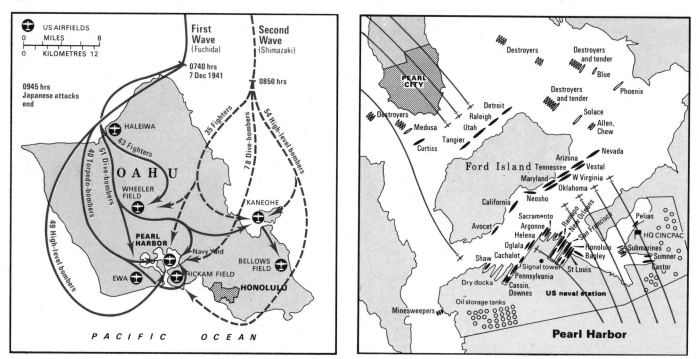

News of the attack at Pearl Harbor was quickly sent to the Philippines where General MacArthur and Admiral Hart alerted all units to prepare for action. Thanks to Admiral Stark's warning of 27 November, defensive preparations had already been initiated but they were still incomplete when the news of the disaster at Pearl Harbor reached Manila at 0230 on 8 December (0800, 7 December, Hawaiian time). This being the case, little could be done in the remaining hours to prevent a repetition of the humiliation suffered at Pearl Harbor. Twice within 24 hours the United States was humbled.

Despite the fact that American military leaders had long considered the possibility of a Japanese attack on the Philippines as a prelude to war between the United States and Japan, defense of the Islands was hopeless from the outset. For years critics and friends of American colonial policy had warned of the weakness of Philippine defenses, but Congress had shown little inclination to appropriate sufficient revenues to allow the establishment of adequate insular protection. Nor had this attitude changed as the likelihood of conflict increased. There was simply no chance of holding the Philippine Islands when the Japanese attacked. The eight-hour warning of possible attack received by MacArthur and Hart before the first Japanese aerial attack on the Philippines might just as well have been eight *minutes*. The battle was lost even before it began.

Japanese planes initiated action against the United States in the Philippines at 0530, 8 December 1941, sinking a seaplane off the coast of Mindanao. Six hours later, Formosa-

Top right : The battleship, *West Virginia*, her hull blackened by fire with pumps ejecting water over the side, is towed to dry dock. Despite the holocaust only two battleships were total losses.
Right : US sailors examine a crashed Japanese Aichi D3A 'Val' dive-bomber.

based bombers attacked American airfields on Luzon destroying dozens of fighters and bombers at Clark, Nichols, Iba and other fields near Manila. Although warnings of the approaching strike force reached Army Air Force headquarters at least 45 minutes before the attack, nothing was done to evacuate the aircraft before the Japanese reached Manila. Japanese pilots found their targets parked like sitting ducks with no anti-aircraft protection. In one day the Far Eastern Air Force of the United States was destroyed just as the Pacific Fleet had been neutralized at Pearl Harbor. Nor was this the only damage wrought by Japanese attackers. The Asiatic Fleet, such as it was, was badly mauled and important dock and repair facilities in the port of Manila were destroyed.

Without aerial and naval strength the American defenders of the Philippines were in no position to resist the Japanese invasion and could not even take effective action to slow the Japanese advance. When amphibious forces were landed on Luzon on 10 December and in other ports during the days that followed, Admiral Hart could not even harass them so small and inadequate was the fleet at his disposal.

Given the hopelessness of the situation, American commanders had little choice but to withdraw from Manila to safer quarters. On 21 December the Navy command moved to Corregidor while on Christmas Eve

Top left: US sailors read the shock headlines of the Pearl Harbor attack.
Above: Japanese troops cheer the capture of a position on Bataan, April 1942.
Top right: Wreckage of burned planes and damaged hangars at Wheeler Field, Hawaii four days after the attack.
Below: The destroyer *Fanning* (DD. 385) and two sister ships underway in the central Pacific in April 1942.

General MacArthur was forced to withdraw to the Bataan peninsula. What remained of the Asiatic Fleet was sent to Java and preparations were made to evacuate leaders of the Philippine Commonwealth to the United States.

By withdrawing to the Bataan Peninsula and Corregidor, MacArthur and Hart hoped to hold out against Japan until reinforcements could be brought to Luzon. This proved impossible given the decimation of the Pacific Fleet and Japan's absolute command of both the Pacific and the air over the Philippine Islands. Although American forces and their Filipino comrades fought bravely, it soon became necessary to abandon even these fortresses. On 11 March 1942 MacArthur reluctantly left the Islands for Australia leaving General Jonathan Wainwright in command. Wainwright held Bataan until 8 April when it became necessary to evacuate to Corregidor. There, the remnants of Wainwright's Army and some Marine units held out for another month but finally succumbed to Japan on 6 May 1942 when Wainwright surrendered Corregidor and all American armed forces in the archipelago to the Japanese. This was the worst defeat in American history to that date. America's inability to hold the Philippines cost tens of thousands of lives and untold billions of dollars and was a disaster which dwarfed the Japanese blitz at Pearl Harbor. Although MacArthur vowed to return and liberate the Islands, it would take him nearly three years to do so.

Army B-25 Mitchell bombers lashed to the flight deck of the carrier *Hornet* (CV. 8) before the Doolittle Raid on Tokyo.

The Tide Turns

46

By the end of March 1942 the Japanese had established the Greater East Asia Co-Prosperity Sphere by force. Burma, the Dutch East Indies, and Malaya were theirs and the Philippines' defenses were rapidly crumbling. If Japan's leaders had remained true to their original war plan, they would have ceased their military offensive, dug in, and awaited diplomatic recognition of the new balance of power in Asia. Such was not to be the case, however, as success whetted the appetite of the warlords in Tokyo, who now began to think of a more complete victory than they had already achieved.

The attack on Pearl Harbor had been carried out according to plan, but despite the havoc wreaked on American forces on Oahu, the Pacific Fleet had not been entirely destroyed. The battleships of the fleet had been sunk or otherwise disabled, but the fleet carriers, having been out of port when the raid occurred, remained intact and still posed a threat to Japanese dominance in the Pacific. If they could be lured into battle and destroyed, Japan's hegemony in East Asia would be assured.

The relative ease with which the Western powers had been defeated

convinced Japan's military leaders that they could modify their original war plan to expand Japan's defensive perimeters without waiting to consolidate earlier gains. Accordingly, a new plan was presented for discussion in March which called for conquest of Tulagi, Port Moresby, Midway Island, the Aleutians, New Caledonia, Fiji and Samoa. This ambitious program was accepted after only cursory discussion and implementation commenced early in April 1942.

In order to annex Tulagi and Port Moresby, possession of which would place Japanese air bases close enough to bomb Australia, the Imperial Navy would have to secure the Coral Sea. Although enemy forces were still reeling from previous attacks the Japanese expected to find some opposition to their New Guinea campaign, but believed that such opposition would be largely limited to land-based air attacks rather than a naval confrontation. This being the case the Coral Sea attack force was modest, consisting of only three carriers, a covering group and naval landing forces. The bulk of Japan's naval forces were being reserved for the Midway campaign.

The Coral Sea operation was under

Left : Lieutenant Colonel James H Doolittle and Admiral Marc Mitscher on board the *Hornet* before the classic raid on Tokyo in April 1942.

Right : A weary pilot of one of the heavy cruiser *Chester*'s (CA. 27) catapult float-planes walks past a gaping hole from a bomb hit on the catapult deck, February 1942.

Below : The Doolittle Raid on Tokyo achieved little of military significance, but dealt a major blow to Japanese morale. Not only was it proof that American naval airpower could strike at the Home Islands but it was also a remarkable achievement to fly twin-engined land bombers from a carrier's deck.

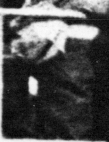

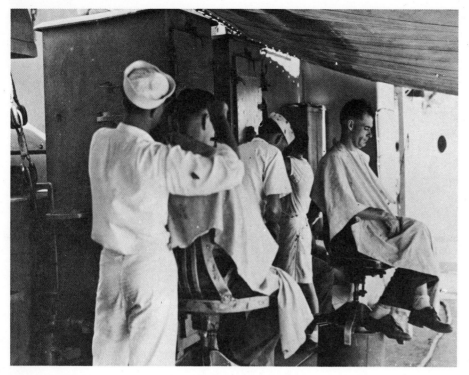

Left: A makeshift barber shop aboard the light cruiser *Marblehead* (CL. 12) in February 1942 after the Battle of the Java Sea.
Right: The *North Carolina* (BB. 55) and her sister *Washington* (BB. 56) were the first of the new generation of fast battleships designed to operate with carrier task forces.

the command of Vice-Admiral Inouye, whose headquarters was located in Rabaul, and was scheduled to begin on 3 May 1942 at which time Tulagi would be occupied. As was so often the case, Japanese strategy in the Battle of the Coral Sea was complex, calling for the division of their forces into three separate groups. As the late Samuel E Morison has pointed out, the successful execution of this plan 'required a tactical competence rare at any time in any Navy, as well as the enemy's passive acceptance of the role he was expected to play.' This was not what happened in May 1942.

Unknown to Japanese leaders American intelligence obtained information about future operations in the

Coral Sea in mid-April. Thus Nimitz and MacArthur were able to conclude correctly that Port Moresby was the major target of Japan's attack and immediately initiated countermeasures that would deny Port Moresby to the enemy. Although Port Moresby lay in MacArthur's 'sphere of jurisdiction,' Nimitz and MacArthur were regarded as co-equal by the Joint Chiefs of Staff in this battle. Nimitz would exercise control of naval operations while MacArthur would be responsible for control of ground forces and land-based aircraft.

America's Coral Sea naval task force was composed of two carriers, the *Yorktown* and the *Lexington*, plus 24 attack, escort, support and supply

ships. It was roughly equal in size to the Japanese force assigned to secure the Coral Sea. Under the overall command of Rear Admiral Frank Fletcher in the *Yorktown*, the American armada was given no specific order by Nimitz other than to 'operate in the Coral Sea commencing on 1 May.' The mechanics of how Fletcher was to prevent the Japanese from obtaining their goals were left to him.

On 1 May 1942 Fletcher's task force assembled, fueled and took on such last minute supplies as were necessary. Fueling was still incomplete the following day when word arrived from General MacArthur that enemy forces were fast approaching their destination. This forced Fletcher to dispatch part of his force including the *Yorktown* to the Coral Sea in case the Japanese arrived there first. The stragglers, including Rear Admiral Fitch in the *Lexington*, were ordered to complete fueling and rendezvous with Fletcher and the *Yorktown* early in the morning of 4 May which would still give the Allied armada sufficient time to intercept the Japanese or so Fletcher thought.

Unknown to the Americans, Admiral Shima's Tulagi Strike Force reached its launching position on 3 May. The nearest American ship was at least 500 miles away. Since the Australian garrison on the island had already been withdrawn, Japanese forces landed on Tulagi without opposition. When word of the Japanese landing finally reached the American command, fueling operations for the *Lexington* force were hastily completed while Fletcher moved northward to close the gap, hoping to bring his Task Force 17 which was composed of the *Yorktown*, three cruisers and six destroyers, within striking distance of Tulagi. He reached his launching position by 0600 on the morning of 4 May.

At 0630 Fletcher launched an attack force of forty planes from the *Yorktown*. Although a considerable tonnage of bombs was dropped, very little significant damage was done. During the early days of carrier warfare in

Left: A 325 lb Mark 17 depth charge is removed from the wing rack of a Curtiss SOC-1 Seagull, on the catapult of the *Philadelphia* (CL. 71).
Right: The destroyer *Aylwin* (DD. 355) receives her first war modifications at Mare Island Navy Yard in March 1942 which included the addition of much-needed 20 mm Oerlikon guns.

Above : The old destroyer *Hatfield* (DD. 231)
was refitted at Puget Sound Navy Yard for
escort work in May 1942.
Below : The destroyer *Callaghan* (DD. 792) as
seen from a carrier.

the Pacific pilots often made mistakes in identifying targets and wasted ammunition on many worthless hits. Fortunately Fletcher and his lieutenants were conservative in their reading of early reports of damage to the Japanese and did not accept the first reports of triumph in the Coral Sea. Had they done so they might have sacrificed what was left of the Pacific Fleet.

Following Fletcher's attack of 4 May there was a two-day interlude during which both sides prepared their forces for a more definitive encounter. Fletcher rendezvoused with Fitch and the *Lexington* on the morning of 5 May while the Japanese Strike Force, under the command of Admiral Takagi and the Support Group, under the command of Rear Admiral Marushige, steamed into the Coral Sea.

By mid-morning on 6 May Japanese carriers had moved deep into the Coral Sea. Although American intelligence provided some information as to the presence of Japanese forces adjacent to the Solomons, land-based reconnaissance planes had failed to spot Takagi's penetration of the Coral Sea – nor was Admiral Fletcher aware that they were steaming towards him in a southerly direction. The Japanese, for their part, were equally ignorant of the position of their enemies and at one point the two fleets came within seventy miles of each other without either side recording an enemy presence.

On the morning of 7 May the much anticipated confrontation in the Coral Sea commenced when Japanese spotters reported sighting an American carrier and a cruiser. In reality it was not a carrier but the oiler *Neosho* and her escort destroyer the *Sims*. At 0930

the Japanese unsuccessfully attacked the two ships, returning for a second attempt about an hour later and a third and final bombing about noon. The *Sims* was hit and sank but the *Neosho* refused to capitulate, drifting at sea for several days before going down. Fortunately for the Americans, the Japanese did not realize their mistaken identity of these vessels for several days. Had they not identified the *Neosho* as the *Yorktown*, they might have continued their search until she was correctly located.

While the *Neosho* and the *Sims* were attempting to ward off their attackers, Fletcher dispatched a task force under the command of Rear Admiral John G Crace, RN, to attack the Port Moresby Invasion Group before it entered the Jomard Passage. 'Crace's chase', as this mission was to become known, turned out to be a comedy of errors. First, Crace's task force was

Above : Four survivors from the oiler *Neosho* (AO. 48) are rescued by a whale boat launched from the destroyer *Helm* (DD. 388). The *Neosho* was mistaken for a carrier during the Coral Sea Battle and was damaged by Japanese planes dispatched by Vice-Admiral Takagi.

attended by Army Air Force pilots who mistakenly identified it as the Port Moresby Invader Group and after successfully outmaneuvering American aviators, Crace's group was then attacked by the Japanese. Miraculously, Crace survived both attacks with minimal damage although Japanese pilots reported having hit a cruiser and a battleship!

As Admiral Crace was attempting to evade his American and Japanese attackers, Admiral Fletcher moved the *Yorktown* to the north, sending out search planes to find the enemy. Shortly after 0800 American planes spotted 'two carriers and four cruisers' and radioed their position back to the

Above : Carrier *Lexington* (CV. 2) maneuvers while under attack from Japanese aircraft during the Battle of Coral Sea, 8 May 1942. She was irreparably damaged in the skirmish.
Left : Douglas Dauntless SBD dive bombers warming up for take off from the carrier *Enterprise* (CV. 6) in the Coral Sea on 8 May 1942.

Yorktown. Within an hour, planes from the *Lexington* were in the air followed shortly by another group from the *Yorktown.* When these missions reached the position where the Japanese were said to be, they found only two light cruisers plus a few gunboats. Once again there had been a breakdown in communications only this time the error was due to a mistaken transcription of the spotter pilot's code pad.

By 0830 Japanese reconnaissance craft pinpointed Fletcher's position and radioed it back to Admiral Goto who ordered planes from the carrier *Shoho* to prepare for attack. However, before these preparations were completed an American scout plane sighted the *Shoho* and her escorts and immediately radioed her position to the returning attack groups from the

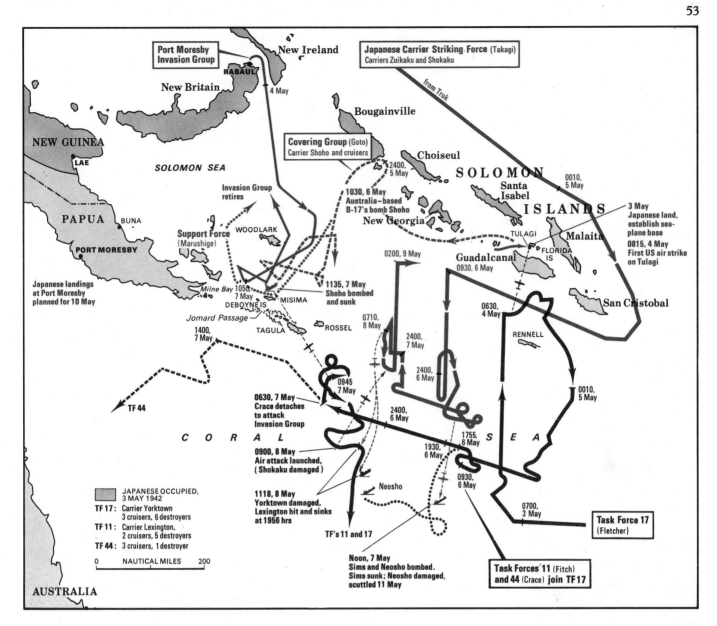

Japanese Carrier Striking Force (Takagi)
Carriers Zuikaku and Shokaku

from Truk

Port Moresby
Invasion Group

New Ireland

RABAUL

New Britain

4 May

Bougainville

Covering Group (Goto)
Carrier Shoho and cruisers

Choiseul

SOLOMON

NEW GUINEA

SOLOMON SEA

Santa
Isabel

0010,
5 May

LAE

ISLANDS

3 May
Japanese land,
establish sea-
plane base

Invasion Group
retires

1030, 6 May
Australia-based
B-17's bomb Shoho

New Georgia

PAPUA

BUNA

WOODLARK

Support Force
(Marushige)

TULAGI

Malaita

0815, 4 May
First US air strike
on Tulagi

PORT MORESBY

FLORIDA
IS

Guadalcanal
0930, 6 May

San Cristobal

Japanese landings
at Port Moresby
planned for 10 May

Milne Bay 1050,
7 May

1135, 7 May
Shoho bombed
and sunk

0200, 9 May

0630,
4 May

RENNELL

DEBOYNE IS

MISIMA

Jomard Passage

0710,
8 May

2400,
7 May

1400,
7 May

TAGULA

ROSSEL

2400,
6 May

0010,
5 May

0945
7 May

2400,
6 May

TF 44

0630, 7 May
Crace detaches
to attack
Invasion Group

2400,
6 May

1755,
6 May

S E A

C O R A L

0900, 8 May
Air attack launched,
(Shokaku damaged)

1930,
6 May

0930,
6 May

0700,
3 May

JAPANESE OCCUPIED,
3 MAY 1942

Neosho

1118, 8 May
Yorktown damaged,
Lexington hit and sinks
at 1956 hrs

TF 17: Carrier Yorktown
3 cruisers, 6 destroyers

TF 11: Carrier Lexington,
2 cruisers, 5 destroyers

TF's 11 and 17

Task Force 17
(Fletcher)

TF 44: 3 cruisers, 1 destroyer

0   NAUTICAL MILES   200

Noon, 7 May
Sims and Neosho bombed.
Sims sunk; Neosho damaged,
scuttled 11 May

Task Forces 11 (Fitch)
and 44 (Crace) join TF 17

AUSTRALIA

Right: Japanese Aichi D3A 'Val' dive bombers ranged on the flight deck of the *Soryu.*

Lexington and the *Yorktown*. They zeroed in on the Japanese carrier, 93 planes strong, and succeeded in putting the *Shoho* under by 1136. '*Scratch one flattop!*' was the message received some few minutes later.

With the loss of the *Shoho* Goto's Cover Group retreated. Admiral Fletcher did not pursue Goto, preferring instead to save his strength for Takagi's main force which had yet to be located. In addition since intercepted messages made it clear that the Japanese had a fix on the *Yorktown* and the *Lexington*, it was imperative they be moved. Accordingly, Fletcher ordered his fleet to proceed toward the Jomard Passage in a westerly direction. As night fell, both sides prepared for their next encounter.

As morning dawned on 8 May each side attempted to locate the other. At 0625 an American search party was sent aloft. About two hours later a similar search mission was launched by the Japanese. American pilots were the first to spot the enemy shortly after

0800. By 0900 the American command had a reasonably accurate fix on Takagi's Strike Force and the first American attack group was taking off from the *Yorktown* at 0915.

At 1100 the *Yorktown* attack group reached the Strike Force and commenced their attack on the carriers *Shokaku* and *Zuikaku*. Shortly thereafter they were joined by planes from the *Lexington*. The *Shokaku* was hit by two bombs but continued to float. A third hit from one of the *Lexington's* planes failed to sink her, although she was sufficiently disabled that her planes had to be transferred to the *Zuikaku*.

Shortly after the beginning of the American attack on the Strike Force, the Japanese commenced their own attack on the *Yorktown* and the *Lexington*. A Japanese counterattack was not unexpected and such being the case, measures had been taken to prepare for it including sending combat patrols aloft to intercept the Japanese. Despite such precautions the Japanese found their mark; the *Lexington* was hit by several torpedoes followed by a devastating bomb attack by Japanese 'Vals.' She was mortally wounded and would be put to her grave at the end of the day. The *Yorktown* was also hit but she was not lost.

The Battle of the Coral Sea was over by midday on 8 May. The Japanese had lost one carrier, several support craft and a second carrier had been seriously damaged. The United States lost one carrier and several support ships, while the *Yorktown* was also damaged. More important, perhaps, was the toll of airplanes lost in the fray. Here the United States fared better than Japan, destroying almost all of the 121 carrier-based aircraft on the two Japanese carriers while sustaining the loss of 76 of their own planes. To be sure, neither side could claim a decisive victory but the United States Navy had held its own against the Japanese, putting to rest the myth of Japan's invincibility.

Top center: The Curtiss SB2C Helldiver was a carrier-based scout bomber which served with distinction in the Pacific from the end of 1943.
Right: A Nakajima B5N 'Kate' bomber attacks a US destroyer during the Battle of the Coral Sea.
Below: The carrier *Shoho* is hit by a torpedo from US bombers from the *Lexington* and *Yorktown* during the Battle of the Coral Sea, 7 May 1942.

Top : Weary .50 cal machine gunners relax after helping to drive off a Japanese air attack.
Above : A *Soryu* Class carrier makes tight evasive turns while under attack from the carrier
Yorktown's aircraft on the morning of 8 May 1942.

Top: The *Lexington* (CV. 2) during the Battle of the Coral Sea. She is down by the bows from her battle damage, but there is no sign yet of the disastrous fire which was to sink her.
Above: The damaged *Lexington* continues to recover her planes, with debris littering the port side gun gallery.
Above right: The internal fires are now out of control and destroyers stand by the stricken carrier to take off personnel.
Below: Closer view of the *Lexington* with a destroyer dimly seen through the clouds of smoke. Scores of crewmen lower themselves into the water down trailing ropes.

Top : The terrible end of the *Lexington* as her shattered hull finally slid under.
Above : A colossal explosion hurls flames and debris overboard, but the destroyer *Hammann* (DD. 412) has just backed clear with a load of survivors.
Above right : This water-damaged photograph of the *Lexington*'s wrecked 5-inch gun battery was retrieved by a survivor.

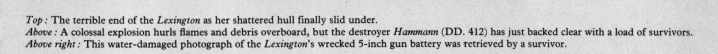

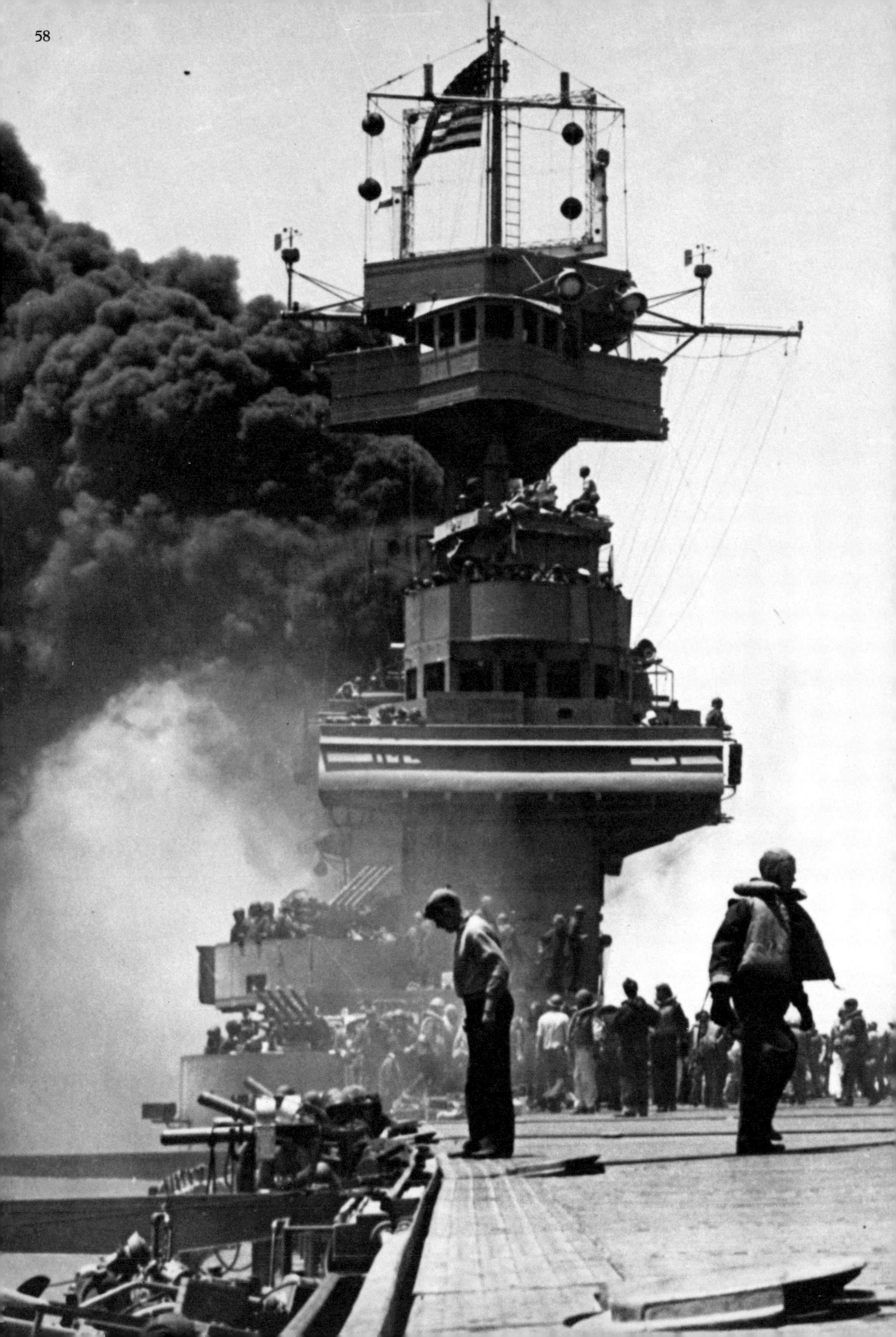

Although the Battle of the Coral Sea was not a decisive encounter, it was unique in the sense that it was the first major naval battle in history in which air power played the major role. Neither the Japanese nor American fleets saw one another nor did one fire upon the other. Guns were employed against enemy aircraft not ships. This was to prove to be the norm and not the exception in this war which witnessed a revolution in strategy and tactics.

If the Battle of the Coral Sea was significant, the Battle of Midway was crucial, for this encounter would determine the future course of the war in the Pacific. Even as the Battle of the Coral Sea was in progress, preparations had commenced in Japan for the effort to seize Midway and destroy what was left of the Pacific Fleet. To accomplish this the Japanese gathered a huge armada of over 200 ships, several times larger than the force committed to the Coral Sea.

The seizure of Midway Island had not been a part of Japan's original war plans. However the success of the initial Japanese campaigns coupled with the Doolittle Raid on Tokyo in April 1942 convinced Japan's military leaders that it was necessary to extend Japan's ribbon defense to Midway

Above left: Five-inch gun crewmen on board the carrier *Yorktown* (CV. 5) play backgammon during a lull in the Battle of Midway.
Left: The *Yorktown*'s fire-fighters silhouetted against the glare of the avgas fires.
Below and opposite: An air of deceptive calm prevails on the flight deck of the *Yorktown* as damage control parties cope with the fires, but the smoke belching from the stack marks a serious bomb hit. However, by 1320 hours she was able to start fueling her fighters once more.

Above: Japanese carrier *Hiryu* wrecked and ablaze during the afternoon of 4 June. The flight deck and hangar in the forward part of the ship have been completely destroyed by bomb hits.
Left: Nakajima B5N 'Kate' carrier-borne torpedo bombers wheel over the *Yorktown*, which is seriously listing from a torpedo hit and is nearly dead in the water.

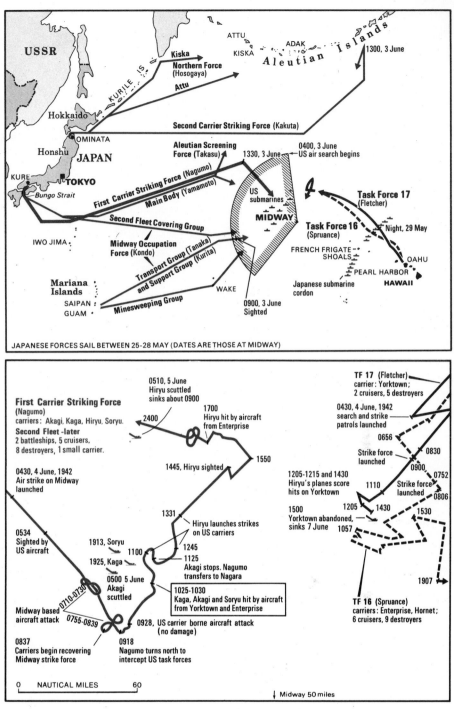

JAPANESE FORCES SAIL BETWEEN 25-28 MAY (DATES ARE THOSE AT MIDWAY)

which could then be used as a base for further attacks on the Hawaiian Islands and, possibly, the west coast of the continental United States. Such an attack would also have the virtue of affording the Japanese another opportunity to decimate the American fleet, for surely the United States would not allow Japan to occupy Midway without a contest.

As conceived by Admiral Yamamoto's staff, the Midway campaign would be carried out in an elaborate series of maneuvers. First, the western Aleutians would be occupied as a diversion to encourage the American command into committing their meager defenses to these northern waters. Second, while the United States bit at Japan's bait off Alaska, an expeditionary force would seize Midway, following which there would be a decisive naval battle off the Island. This last phase would destroy the Pacific Fleet. To accomplish his ends, Yamamoto divided his forces into five

Far left: Douglas SBD Dauntless during the Battle of Midway flies over the smoke trail left by the burning light cruiser *Mikuma*, a member of the *Mogami* Class which were laid down in the 1930s.
Left: A crippled Douglas SBD Dauntless crashes into the sea near a heavy cruiser during the Battle of Midway.

units, each responsible for executing an elaborate game plan which had become the rule of thumb for Japanese operations.

The success of Yamamoto's Midway plan depended upon surprising the enemy. Indeed, it was expected that Midway would be taken with little or no opposition! Such was not to be the case, however, for once again American intelligence had pieced together a sufficient picture of Japanese intent to alert Nimitz and his staff that something big was brewing. By the time that Yamamoto was ready to dispatch his armada, Nimitz had relatively detailed knowledge of enemy forces, their disposition and destination. Accordingly the United States Navy was prepared to take maximum advantage of minimal resources to deny the Japanese a victory at Midway.

Early in May 1942 Nimitz and his staff assessed the resources available to them to confront the Japanese. They were meager at best. Compared to the Japanese task force which contained at least seven carriers, several battleships, and dozens of other support craft, Nimitz could count on only three carriers, the *Saratoga,* the *Enterprise* and the *Hornet.* The *Lexington* had been lost in the Coral Sea and the *Yorktown* had been mauled there as well. Were it not for the fact that the Japanese would divide their forces into five groups, diluting their strength, Nimitz might have given up from the start, but knowing of the complicated deployment of enemy forces, he was able to realistically devise a successful defensive strategy.

On 27 May Nimitz announced his

Above : The carrier *Yorktown* is surrounded by shell-bursts from her own and her escort's anti-aircraft barrage.
Below : Once again a destroyer helps to evacuate personnel from a sinking carrier as the *Yorktown* nears the end of her struggle to stay afloat at Midway.

operation plan to members of his staff. Midway's garrison was to be reinforced and new search radar equipment installed immediately. Carriers under the command of Admirals Fletcher and Spruance were to be deployed northeast of Midway where they would be beyond the range of Japanese reconnaissance aircraft. Midway-based aircraft were to carry out regular sweeps in search of the enemy. All American units were to take 'calculated risks' to inflict maximum damage on the enemy *but* commanders were ordered to avoid encounters which would put their forces in danger unless there were significant opportunities to inflict greater damage on the Japanese then they might receive. Above all, every reasonable effort was to be made to avoid detection and thus surprise Yamamoto.

As the Japanese approached Midway the Americans completed their preparations and stood waiting for the enemy. They did not have long to wait. On 3 June a naval reconnaissance pilot spotted Admiral Kondo's Occupation Force some 700 miles away from Midway. Later that day additional sitings were made and a group of B-17s attacked what were reported as several battleships and/or heavy cruisers. It was not until the next day, however, that the battle commenced in earnest.

Above left : A bomb hit on the *Yorktown*'s island superstructure blew out most of her boiler fires.
Left : A Nakajima B5N 'Kate' torpedo bomber turns away from the *Yorktown* after an attack on the doomed carrier. Eventually the Japanese submarine *I. 168* torpedoed her. She sunk at 0501, 7 June.

On 4 June Admiral Nagumo, Commander of the Carrier Strike Force, ordered 108 planes to attack Midway. He was unaware of the presence of the *Enterprise* and the *Hornet* some 300 miles ENE of the Island and had even less notion that the *Yorktown*, presumed dead in the Coral Sea, had been resurrected. His position, on the other hand, was known to Fletcher and Spruance who prepared to move in for the kill.

Nagumo's planes reached Midway shortly after 0600 where they were met by a Marine fighter squadron. Greatly outnumbered, the Marines failed to stop the attack. Japanese bombers pierced Midway's defenses dropping their loads at about 0630. The Japanese attack caused considerable damage but the airstrip remained usable. The Japanese retreated before 0700, ostensibly to refuel and return for a second and final attack. Nagumo still did not know the whereabouts of the American carriers. It was not until after the second attack mission was on its way back to Midway that American ships were spotted NE of the Island.

The discovery of American naval vessels, including at least one aircraft carrier, posed a major problem. Nagumo's attack group was already heading for a second round over Midway. With his planes flying towards Midway, Nagumo could not protect his task force without changing course but to do so would jeopardize the attack on Midway. After some hesitation Nagumo chose to alter course. This decision was made none too soon for at that very moment the Americans were closing in on his fleet.

When the first wave of American aircraft reached the place where Nagumo's forces were supposed to be they found nothing there and by the time they caught the Japanese, Nagumo was prepared for the attack. The first group of American planes were successfully repulsed, many of the bombers being shot down within close range of Japanese ships. As the Americans retreated Nagumo and his aides breathed a sigh of relief, but unknown to them the worst was yet to come.

Since the Japanese had spotted only one American carrier, Nagumo might well have expected the battle to be over and could not have been prepared for a second wave of attackers from the *Enterprise* and the *Yorktown* which were rapidly closing in for the kill. 37 American planes reached their prey shortly after 1000. The US pilots had a clear view of Nagumo's four carriers which were still firing at the retreating American torpedo planes. Minutes later the second attack commenced.

The *Akagi*, Nagumo's flagship, was hit at 1026 and shortly thereafter the ship had to be abandoned. Two other carriers, the *Kaga* and the *Soryu*, were also hit and suffered the same fate as the *Akagi*. Only the carrier *Hiryu* remained afloat, her planes making a successful counterattack on the *Yorktown*. But by the end of the day she too was destroyed, giving the Americans a toll of four carriers at the cost of only one of theirs, the *Yorktown*.

Having lost all of his carriers Admiral Nagumo was relieved of his command by Yamamoto who still labored under the delusion that the

Left : The Japanese heavy cruiser *Mikuma* is seen from a US dive bomber and appears to be abandoned and sinking.
Below left : Underway in March 1934 this submarine, later called the *I. 168*, sank the aircraft carrier *Yorktown* (CV. 5) and the destroyer *Hammann* (DD. 412) during the Battle of Midway. Even so, the Battle of Midway destroyed the Japanese mastery of the sea. The US had turned the tide.

Americans had but one carrier in the vicinity of Midway. Yamomoto proposed to move his Main Force up to replace the Striking Force which had been virtually destroyed. The Aleutian Task Force was ordered to join the Main Force off Midway as quickly as possible for a joint attack on Midway the next day. It was only after the Japanese learned of the existence of other American carriers, thanks to information relayed by pilots returning to the *Hiryu* that evening, that plans for a counteroffensive were modified and later canceled. For all purposes the Battle of Midway had been decided on 4 June.

The decimation of Nagumo's Task Force prevented the Japanese occupation of Midway which had originally been scheduled to begin on 5 June. Early in the morning on that day Admiral Yamamoto sadly ordered Admiral Kurita's Support Group to

Below left : The anti-aircraft cruiser *Atlanta* (CL. 51) steams to the assistance of the destroyer *Phelps* (DD. 360) during the Battle of Midway, while the carrier *Hornet* (CV. 8) and her heavy cruiser escort *New Orleans* (CA. 32) continue the futile chase to catch Admiral Yamamoto and his fast-disappearing fleet.
Below : Having inspected its depths Admiral Chester Nimitz leaves a bunker on Midway Island some time after the battle.

cease its bombardment of Midway installations and regain the fleet. Shortly thereafter and unknown to Fletcher and Spruance, Yamamoto ordered the forces under his command to retire from Midway to safer waters.

Had the American command realised the extent of the physical and psychological damage they had inflicted on the Japanese perhaps they would have pursued them with greater vigor, preventing Yamamoto from returning without significant losses, but for the moment prudence dictated caution. The Japanese still possessed significant fire power and had reinforcements coming from the Aleutians. Given these facts and the inexperience of American pilots with night missions, Spruance decided to steam away from the Japanese and wait until daybreak on 5 June before pursuing the enemy by which time the Japanese had retreated too far to the west. Although both sides were involved in minor skirmishes during the next day or two, the Battle of Midway came to an end on 5 June.

Midway marked a turning point in the War. Six months after their attack on Pearl Harbor the Japanese were forced on the defensive. From June 1942 until August 1945 the Japanese continued their retreat to the west, never again regaining the momentum of the first months of the war. Although it would take an additional two years and countless thousands of lives to defeat Japan, the die had been cast at Midway. In retrospect the Battle for Midway was not simply an American naval victory, it was one of the watersheds of World War II.

Japanese dead on Guadalcanal, one of the most bloody battlefields of the Pacific war.

Watchtower-the Test

68

The American victory at Midway convinced Marshall and King that it might be possible to move from a defensive to an offensive posture, carrying the war towards Japan for the first time. Such views were enthusiastically advanced by field commanders such as MacArthur and Nimitz who were eager to avenge earlier humiliations. Although they recognized the futility of trying to persuade the Roosevelt administration to abandon its primary commitment to defeat Germany, MacArthur, Nimitz and their supporters at the Pentagon presented convincing evidence of the opportunity at hand. The question was no longer whether to take advantage of the momentum of the Battle of Midway but, rather, how to do so. Here the senior field commanders were in disagreement.

As might have been expected, Admirals King and Nimitz saw the Navy playing the major role in new offensives against Japan. This was strategically appropriate because of the nature of the Pacific Theater. MacArthur, on the other hand, did not share his colleagues' conception of naval strategy and/or justice and refused to hear of any plan which did not permit *his* command to extract its pound of flesh from the Japanese as an equal of the naval forces under the jurisdiction of Nimitz.

There was a protracted debate between MacArthur, Nimitz and their respective supporters until a com-

promise was worked out by the Joint Chiefs of Staff early in July. This plan called for a three-stage initiative against Japan and divided responsibility between the two services in the following manner: during Phase I, the Navy would be responsible for the occupation of the eastern Solomon Islands, particularly Guadalcanal and Tulagi, and the Santa Cruz group; during Phase II, MacArthur's forces would complete the occupation of the Solomons and land on New Guinea; during Phase III, MacArthur's forces would neutralize Rabaul, Japan's most important base in the South Pacific.

It has often been said that a compromise is reached when both parties to a matter under litigation leave the table unsatisfied. This was most certainly the case regarding the decision of the Joint Chiefs on 2 July described above. Nimitz resented the ambitious role assigned to MacArthur; MacArthur resented the over-cautiousness of the whole offensive. Both men, however, understood that if they failed to accept this compromise, there might well be no action against Japan at that time; so it was that they gave their mixed blessings to the venture.

'Operation Watchtower,' the codename given to the Pacific offensive, called for the Navy to assure access to New Britain, New Guinea and New Ireland by securing the Santa Cruz and Solomon Islands. Preparations for this effort began early in August

1942. Contingency plans for such an operation had actually been developed months before the Joint Chiefs' 2 July mandate but as is so often the case in war, unanticipated events forced a change in pace and plans.

Within days after the promulgation of Operation Watchtower American and Allied intelligence reported that Japanese forces were building an airstrip on Guadalcanal, one of the

Top left : Admiral John McCain (right) and
Major General Alexander Vandegrift on an
American base in the Solomons.
Above : Marine raiders leave for Guadalcanal
from an old destroyer converted to a fast
transport (APD).
Right : Japanese Marines prepare for the
invasion of Guadalcanal. The situation looked
considerably less peaceful once the US Marines
attacked.
Below : Mitsubishi G4M 'Betty' heavy bombers
come in low over Guadalcanal to attack US
vessels on 8 August 1942.

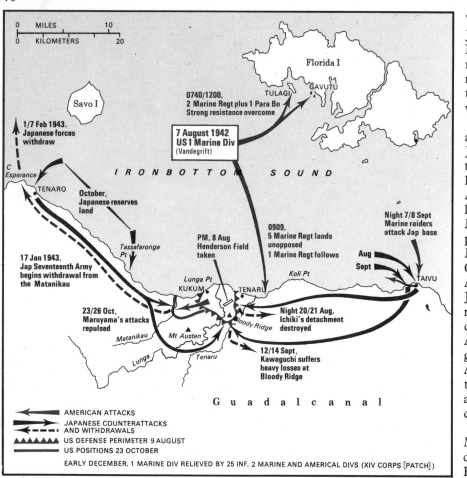

0 MILES 10
0 KILOMETERS 20

Florida I

TULAGI GAVUTU

0740/1200,
2 Marine Regt plus 1 Para Bn
Strong resistance overcome

Savo I

7 August 1942
US 1 Marine Div
(Vandegrift)

1/7 Feb 1943,
Japanese forces
withdraw

I R O N B O T T O M   S O U N D

C
Esperance

TENARO

October,
Japanese reserves
land

Night 7/8 Sept
Marine raiders
attack Jap base

0909,
5 Marine Regt lands
unopposed
1 Marine Regt follows

PM, 8 Aug
Henderson Field
taken

Aug
Sept

TAIVU

Tassafaronga
Pt

Koli Pt

17 Jan 1943,
Jap Seventeenth Army
begins withdrawal from
the Matanikau

Lunga Pt
KUKUM

TENARU

Night 20/21 Aug,
Ichiki's detachment
destroyed

23/26 Oct,
Maruyama's attacks
repulsed

Bloody Ridge

Matanikau

Mt Austen

12/14 Sept,
Kawaguchi suffers
heavy losses at
Bloody Ridge

Lunga

Tenaru

G u a d a l c a n a l

AMERICAN ATTACKS
JAPANESE COUNTERATTACKS
AND WITHDRAWALS
US DEFENSE PERIMETER 9 AUGUST
US POSITIONS 23 OCTOBER

EARLY DECEMBER, 1 MARINE DIV RELIEVED BY 25 INF, 2 MARINE AND AMERICAL DIVS (XIV CORPS [PATCH])

largest islands at the southeast end of the Solomons chain. If this field was completed before the commencement of Phase I of the American offensive, the success of the entire venture would be jeopardized. Accordingly, Nimitz ordered Admiral Ghormley to seize Guadalcanal and Tulagi by no later than the middle of August.

Given the timetable under which Nimitz and his subordinates were working, there was little time for planning or preparation. An *ad hoc*

task force was hastily to be assembled at the end of July for the purpose of carrying a landing party of Marines to Guadalcanal for the first amphibious operation of the war. This amphibious force was placed under the command of Rear Admiral Richmond Kelly Turner. D-Day for the landing was to be 7 August 1942.

The first group of Marines was landed on Guadalcanal early on 7 August. By the end of the day some 11,000 men had established a safe beachhead just east of Lunga Point.

Within 24 hours they captured the Japanese airfield, soon to be renamed Henderson Field, meeting very little resistance from Japanese forces who retreated into the steaming interior of the island rather than fight. All went well, perhaps too well.

There is little doubt that Turner's amphibious landing caught the Japanese by surprise and knocked them off balance. Unfortunately this loss of equilibrium was only temporary. As soon as word of the American landings reached Rabaul, Admiral Mikawa immediately commenced preparations for a countermove. Mikawa's response to Phase I of Operation Watchtower was twofold. An effort was made to reinforce the Japanese garrison on Guadalcanal by running transports and their escorts down the Slot between the Solomons. At the same time, a task force was gathered and dispatched to engage American naval forces off the coast of the island. This was to be a surprise attack carried out under cover of darkness.

During the night of 8–9 August Mikawa's task force of cruisers and destroyers entered Ironbottom Sound. By that time Admiral Fletcher had ordered the *Saratoga*, the *Wasp*, and the *Enterprise* to retire from Guadalcanal on the basis of intelligence reports of Japanese movements toward the area, thus leaving Turner's force unprotected by air cover. Such ships as Turner had at his disposal were assigned to one of three patrol zones in anticipation of a Japanese attack. In the meanwhile transport and supply vessels continued to unload their cargoes lest the Marines find themselves stranded on Guadalcanal with inadequate stores and rations before the transports followed the example of Fletcher's carriers and left the area on 9 August.

Mikawa's ships were not equipped with radar but thanks to escort planes, the Japanese were aware of the disposition of the American Fleet and ready to launch torpedo attacks against the enemy. The first target for this attack was to be the cruiser screen just off the landing area, the second was to be the transports. Mikawa planned to retreat quickly after the attack before Fletcher's carrier group was able to maneuver within striking distance of the Japanese attack force.

Shortly after 0130 on 9 August Mikawa ordered his men to attack the Americans who were still unaware of the presence of his fleet. Minutes

Left : One of the three US heavy cruisers of the *Astoria* Class seen in the glare of Japanese searchlights as she sinks during the Battle of Savo Island on 9 August 1942.

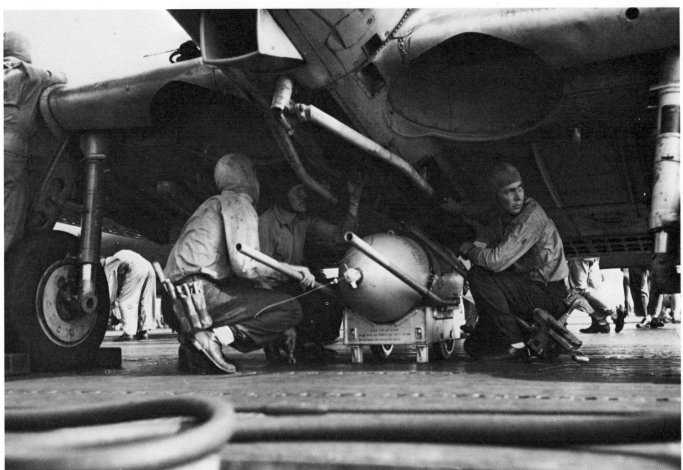

Above : Flight deck crew of the carrier *Enterprise* (CV. 6) load a 500lb bomb under a Douglas SBD Dauntless for the attack on Guadalcanal.
Right : A sandwich break for a Marine anti-aircraft crew aboard the *Wasp* (CV. 7). Their 20mm Oerlikon gun soon went back into action during the naval Battle of Guadalcanal.

later the destroyer *Patterson* sighted the Japanese and sounded an alert. However, by this time it was already too late for the Americans to protect themselves against the enemy. The Battle of Savo Island had begun.

At 0142 Japanese planes dropped flares over Turner's task force and launched torpedoes a minute later. The cruiser *Canberra* was almost instantly hit, followed quickly by the *Patterson*, the *Chicago*, the *Astoria*, the *Quincy*, the *Vincennes* and the *Talbot*. Surprisingly, Mikawa ordered his forces to withdraw at 0220. Perhaps he did not realize that Fletcher's carrier group was not in the vicinity. In any case this somewhat hasty retreat spared the transports from destruction. Considering the disarray of the American command and the chaos of the situation it would not have been difficult to maul the transports and support ships.

The Battle of Savo Island was a disaster for the United States Navy. Seven ships were destroyed or damaged and 1800 men were killed or wounded at almost no cost to the enemy. Such losses seriously eroded

Above: US amphibious transports seen over the starboard floatplane of the heavy cruiser USS *Chicago* (CA. 29) as they leave Tulagi on 10 August 1942.
Above right: The destroyer *Buchanan* (DD. 484) with a damaged bow after the Battle of Kolombangara.
Below: US transports burn off Guadalcanal after a Japanese air raid.

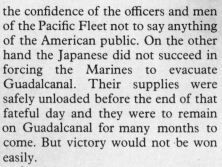

the confidence of the officers and men of the Pacific Fleet not to say anything of the American public. On the other hand the Japanese did not succeed in forcing the Marines to evacuate Guadalcanal. Their supplies were safely unloaded before the end of that fateful day and they were to remain on Guadalcanal for many months to come. But victory would not be won easily.

Guadalcanal was to prove a hell for General Vandegrift and his Marine garrison. Supplies remained a problem for many months, enemy harassment was an almost daily affair and the work required to create Henderson Field was particularly difficult given the climatic conditions in the Solomons. Without adequate naval support forces in the area the Marines were virtually isolated. Such material as was made available was barely enough to meet their immediate needs and certainly not sufficient to allow Vandegrift to pursue an offensive against the enemy.

Shortly after the Battle of Savo Island the Japanese escalated their effort to run troops from Rabaul to Guadalcanal. Fortunately for the Americans Japanese estimates of enemy troop strength were too low and accordingly they did not initially send adequate reinforcements to threaten US control of Henderson Field, which became vitually operational on 17 August. On the other hand regular aerial and naval bombardment of the area made life miserable for the American garrison.

Above : Crew members of the *O'Bannon* (DD. 450) await orders 22 August 1943 during the campaign in the central Solomons. Launched in March 1942, the *O'Bannon* was one of thirty *Fletcher* Class destroyers.

It soon became clear to the Japanese that a major effort would be required to dislodge the Marines from Guadalcanal. Such an effort was discussed and sanctioned on 21 August at a meeting of Japanese military and naval leaders in Rabaul. According to this plan, Operation Ka, a massive naval task force was to be assembled and dispatched in the Solomons to destroy American naval strength in the area, following which additional reinforcements would be landed to augment the Japanese garrison on the island reparatory to a full scale assault on Henderson Field.

Allied intelligence became aware of an unusual concentration of enemy forces prior to 24 August, the designated D-Day for the Japanese

Below : Anti-aircraft fire from ships off the Guadalcanal landing beaches, August 1942.
Far right, bottom : US Marines take a brief respite during the Battle of Guadalcanal, August 1942.

offensive. Accordingly Ghormley instructed Fletcher and other subordinates to keep the shipping lanes into the area open and ordered a large force to assemble south of Guadalcanal to facilitate the accomplishment of this mission. This force included the carriers *Enterprise, Hornet, Saratoga* and *Wasp* plus the battleships *Washington* and *South Dakota*.

As usual the Japanese divided their fleet into several groups according to yet another complicated plan. Admiral Kondo, to whom was entrusted Japan's fate in this Battle of the Eastern Solomons, hoped to lure American forces away from Guadalcanal by offering the light cruiser *Ryujo* as bait in a manner reminiscent of Japanese strategy at Midway. While the Americans moved to take this bait Japanese flyers would launch a devastating attack on Henderson Field, 1500 Japanese would be landed on Guadalcanal and carrier-based aircraft would decimate the enemy who suspected nothing of the presence of Japanese naval forces beyond the *Ryujo* task force.

American reconnaissance planes

Above : Marines dig in around Henderson Field on Guadalcanal during the fall of 1942. The purpose of this operation was to construct a defense perimeter around the airstrip to prevent Japanese raiders from interdicting the flow of material through sporadic raids.
Top right : A bomb explodes just aft of the island of the *Enterprise* (CV. 6) in the Battle of the Eastern Solomons, August 1942. This remarkable photograph was taken from the camera of a dead photographer, who must have been killed by the same blast.

spotted the *Ryujo* and her protectors shortly after 0900 on 24 August. This report was confirmed by another spotter some 2.5 hours later. The *Enterprise* and the *Saratoga* were soon directed to engage the enemy. As planes on both carriers were being readied for an attack against the *Ryujo*, word was received of the presence of two other Japanese carriers, the *Shokaku* and the *Zuikaku*, less than 250 miles away. Unfortunately this news did not reach Fletcher or Kinkaid promptly. By the time it did they had already launched a first wave of planes and were unable to abort these missions in order to take full precautionary measures against the forthcoming enemy attack.

76

Left : Interested members of the crew watch Japanese naval prisoners of war board the light cruiser *San Juan* (CL. 54), 16 October 1942. The Japanese gentleman in the right foreground was an officer who later tried to commit hara-kiri. The attempt was unsuccessful.

The *Ryujo* had served as a sacrificial lamb by 2000 hours but there the Japanese scenario ended. What followed was improvised by both sides. When Japanese pilots arrived above the *Enterprise* at about 1630, they were met by a combat air patrol and a barrage of anti-aircraft flak. Despite this fact the *Enterprise* was hit by several bombs but remained afloat. The *North Carolina*, stationed about two miles away from the *Enterprise*, was also attacked but not hit. The Japanese retreated by 1650, erroneously thinking that the *Enterprise* had been destroyed. A second wave of attackers did not discover the *Enterprise*, temporarily incapacitated while repair crews quickly worked to restore rudder control. The *Saratoga* escaped attack and was able to launch her own counterattack, hitting the seaplane carrier *Chitose* at approximately 1745 before her planes returned. Shortly after this both sides retired from the battle.

The following day, 25 August, the *Wasp* rejoined her sisters after refueling and sent scout planes aloft to find the enemy. But there was no enemy to be found as Kondo had withdrawn his task force to Rabaul. This ended the Battle of the Eastern Solomons. Although neither side could claim victory the Japanese had not been able to land reinforcements on Guadalcanal. In that sense Ghormley won something more than a Pyrrhic victory.

After the Battle of the Eastern Solomons the Japanese temporarily gave up their effort to engage the Americans in a decisive encounter. Instead they reinforced their garrison on Guadalcanal by running small nightly convoys down the Slot. These became known as the Tokyo Express. By day the United States ruled the waves adjacent to the island and this peculiar stalemate prevailed for weeks.

Except for a Japanese submarine attack on the *Saratoga* on 31 August which caused sufficient damage to lay her up for several weeks, there was no change in the *status quo* on Guadalcanal. The Marines continued to hold the territory but the Japanese continued to reinforce their garrison using the Tokyo Express. If such reinforcements could not be stopped it was questionable whether Operation Watchtower could ever succeed. Unless something was done to break the stalemate there could be no further progress towards the capture of Rabaul.

American frustration with the situation on Guadalcanal was exacerbated by the loss of the carrier *Wasp* at the hands of Japanese sub-

Above : A Japanese bomb splashes astern of the
carrier *Hornet* as an enemy plane pulls out of
its dive above the carrier in the Battle of
Santa Cruz.
Below : The *Hornet* (CV. 8) ablaze during the
Battle of Santa Cruz. Destroyers stand by.

marines on 15 September. Nor was *Wasp* the only ship attacked by I-Boats. The *North Carolina* and the *Hornet* were also targets for Japanese torpedoes. Fortunately, they escaped unharmed. The only bright spot for the Americans during the month was the arrival of 4000 Marine reinforcements on 18 September.

The success with which the Tokyo Express carried reinforcements to Guadalcanal had a profound impact upon the morale of Vandegrift's men, who became increasingly bitter about and critical of the Navy's seeming unwillingness to contest Japan's nighttime control of the waters off Guadalcanal. Even the 'victory' of Admiral Scott in the Battle of Cape Esperance (11–12 October) failed to buoy spirits because it represented only a temporary cessation of Japanese movement down the Slot. Only three days later the Japanese were brazenly unloading troops and supplies within sight of the Americans.

Early in October Army men from the American division began to replace the original Marine landing force which was returned to Hawaii to enjoy a well-earned period of rest and recreation. The Army men were quickly introduced to the daily hell of life near Henderson Field when a force of Japanese cruisers and battleships launched a particularly devastating night bombardment of the airstrip on 19 October. Bombardment from naval vessels and/or aircraft was nothing new in Guadalcanal but their visit nearly destroyed Henderson Field and further daunted American spirits.

By the middle of October the situation on Guadalcanal was such that Nimitz began to wonder whether the island could be held without committing more aid to the American garrison. In the light of the upcoming

operation in North Africa and plans for a cross-Channel offensive in 1943 it would be difficult to find such assistance, but if this was not done the whole Solomons campaign would have to be sacrificed. To men like MacArthur and Nimitz this was unthinkable. Thanks to their lobbying, President Roosevelt and the Joint Chiefs were persuaded not to abandon Operation Watchtower and a renewed commitment to reinforce the garrison at Guadalcanal was made at the end of the month.

As part of the effort to bolster the sagging morale of those involved in the battle for Guadalcanal and to break the stalemate in the Solomons, a change of command was ordered for the South Pacific. On 16 October Nimitz announced that Admiral Ghormley was to be replaced as COMSOPAC by Vice-Admiral William F Halsey. Halsey had the reputation of being an aggressive

commander of considerable spunk and spirit. It was hoped some of the spirit might rub off on his subordinates. To give Halsey a good start and some 'teeth,' the battleship *Indiana* was ordered into the Pacific and the carrier *Enterprise* was returned to the Solomons following completion of repairs of damages she had suffered in August. In addition 24 submarines were sent to join Halsey's fleet. These reinforcements arrived none too soon, for towards the end of October the Japanese were planning yet another effort to destroy American naval forces in the vicinity of Guadalcanal.

On 23 October Admiral Yamamoto instructed subordinates to assemble a vast task force for purposes of engaging and annihilating the enemy and capturing Henderson Field. Consisting of four carriers, two battleships, ten cruisers and over two dozen destroyers, the Japanese fleet was to be assisted by land-based aircraft and

Far left: Task Force 16 takes evasive action under Japanese attack in the Battle of Santa Cruz. Large ships in the foreground are the *Portland* (CA. 33) and the *South Dakota* (BB. 57) and obscured by smoke is the *Enterprise.*

Left: A Japanese dive bomber is about to crash into the signal bridge of the USS *Hornet* as she heels in a tight turn during the Battle of Santa Cruz.
Below: A plane hits the bridge of the *Hornet* sending debris into the sea.

submarines. Against this armada Halsey mustered an equally impressive force of two carriers, two battleships, nine cruisers and 24 destroyers – a fleet almost equal to that of the enemy.

Fortunately for Halsey American intelligence provided critical information about enemy movements before the Japanese were able to get a fix on his forces. This gave the United States an important edge in the Battle of the Santa Cruz Islands, as this encounter was to become known. But advance information did not guarantee victory.

The Battle of the Santa Cruz Islands commenced on the morning of 26 October by which time the Japanese had ascertained the presence of Halsey's fleet and its relative disposition. The Japanese were first to launch an air strike, at about 0700, followed closely by American planes

launched from the *Enterprise* and the *Hornet*. As the battle progressed it became a duel between carrier groups and aircraft with capital ships playing a minor role.

The *Hornet* was first to be struck, receiving several bomb hits after 1910. Japanese torpedoes dropped from low-flying Kates also found their mark. Within fifteen minutes after being attacked, the *Hornet* was immobilized, her engines dead and her communication systems out of order. Repair and salvage crews valiantly sought to repair the damage to the ship but renewed Japanese attacks on this vessel rendered their efforts hopeless. Some six hours after she had first been hit, the *Hornet* had to be abandoned.

At about the same time as the *Hornet* was first attacked, 52 of her planes approached the enemy carriers

Shokaku and *Zuiho* and commenced an attack of their own. The *Shokaku* was almost immediately hit and she was rendered useless to the Japanese fleet for several months. The *Zuiho* was also hit. A second wave of planes from the *Hornet* disabled the cruiser *Chikuma* but failed to administer the *coup de grâce* to the two Japanese carriers.

It was only after the first round of action on 26 October that the Japanese learned of the presence of the *Enterprise*, a ship they had believed lay at the bottom of the ocean. With two carriers of their own still functional, a decision was hastily made to put the *Enterprise* out of commission. By 1000 Japanese planes were ready to strike and strike they did only minutes later. Several bombs hit the *Enterprise* but thanks to her new anti-aircraft

Above : Survivors of the *Hornet* (CV. 8) are taken off by a destroyer after the Battle of Santa Cruz, 26 October 1942.
Below : Plane-handling crews at work on the *Enterprise* (CV. 6) during the Battle of Santa Cruz.
Bottom right : The forward 5-inch and 1.1-inch guns of the anti-aircraft cruiser *San Juan* (CL. 54) during a lull in the Battle of Santa Cruz. In the background heavy flak surrounds the *Hornet* as she is attacked by the ships of the Imperial Japanese Navy.

equipment and support from neighboring vessels, the Japanese were not able to complete their kill. The *Enterprise* remained afloat and functional, launching additional air strikes later in the day.

The Battle of the Santa Cruz Islands ended the next morning, 27 October, when both sides retired to count casualties and nurse wounds. Neither side had won a victory in this battle. Indeed the situation on Guadalcanal remained the same as it had been before 26 October – a stalemate. About all that might be said about the encounter from an American perspective was that additional time had been bought to reinforce the garrison and the Japanese had failed in their effort to destroy Henderson Field.

As November dawned it seemed to the Americans that there might never

Left: The abandoned and burned-out *Hornet* was torpedoed by Japanese aircraft and the destroyers the *Akigumo* and *Mukigumo* after Santa Cruz, October 1942. The splash in the right foreground was caused by a torpedo which was dropped by a Japanese plane. The *Hornet* sunk at 1015, 26 October.
Below left: A Douglas SBD Dauntless is blown off the deck of the USS *Enterprise* during the Battle of Santa Cruz.

be an end to the Guadalcanal debacle. Frustration was rampant, even affecting Admiral Halsey who had only been on the job for several weeks. But this frustration was not limited to the Americans. Yamamoto and his underlings were equally vexed and humiliated by their inability to move events off dead center. Incidentally Halsey and Yamamoto concluded that something decisive had to be done and unknown to the other, both Admirals prepared for yet another battle.

Halsey hoped to reinforce the American garrison on Guadalcanal to the point where it could begin an overland offensive to remove the Japanese from their pocket on the island. Beginning on 30 October and continuing for almost two weeks thereafter American ships carried men and material to the island on a daily basis. Ironically the Japanese were doing precisely the same thing and Halsey's efforts to saturate Japanese positions with naval and land-based artillery did little to halt the enemy's efforts.

On or before 10 November Halsey received intelligence reports of a massive enemy build-up at Rabaul and Truk which led him to the inescapable conclusion that Yamamoto was making one last effort to break up the deadlock. Determined that the United States would not be overpowered or beaten to the punch, Halsey brought together all of the strength at his disposal in the South Pacific and charged his subordinates, Kinkaid, Lee and Turner with holding the line. The enemy was also prepared. Thanks to his own intelligence Yamamoto had an equally good fix on the Americans. Unlike previous encounters the Naval Battle of Guadalcanal allowed neither side to take advantage of a surprise attack.

By 12 November both sides were converging off Guadalcanal but action did not commence until the next morning at 0141 when Vice-Admiral Abe's Raiding Group unexpectedly ran into Rear Admiral Daniel Callaghan's Support group off the north coast of Guadalcanal, almost midway between Lunga Point and Cape Espérance. Since the Americans generally returned from unsafe waters after nightfall, Abe had not expected to find any Americans in this area and was not prepared for an encounter. On the other hand the Americans were not well prepared for night action and lost precious time before opening fire.

Callaghan ordered his forces to open fire on the enemy at 0145 but there was considerable confusion on the American side as to the position of enemy ships. What followed was one of the strangest naval duels of the war with both sides engaged in small dogfights which were intermittently broken off for fear that vessels were firing upon friendly vessels and not the enemy. The fray came to an end about an hour after Abe ordered his battleships to return to the north at 0200. During this brief encounter the United States lost the cruisers *Atlanta* and *Juneau* and the destroyers *Barton*, *Cushing*, *Laffey* and *Monssen*. The Japanese lost destroyers *Akatsuki* and *Yudachi*. In addition several other destroyers were hit or damaged as was the battleship *Hiei* which was sunk the next day by American planes.

Despite the losses suffered by Callaghan's support group before his own untimely death on the night of 13 November, its mission to prevent the Japanese from putting Henderson Field out of commission was a success. Abe was not able to turn one gun on Henderson Field, but much remained to be done by the Americans for the Japanese were still determined to reinforce their garrison on the island.

On the morning of 14 November American search planes spotted a large Japanese task force steaming down the Slot. Since aircraft from the *Enterprise* were already busy trying to decimate Admiral Mikawa's retreating support group, Henderson Field based aircraft were sent aloft to batter this

Below: The heavy cruiser *New Orleans* (CA. 32) was camouflaged after the Battle of Tassafaronga at Tulagi to give repair-parties time to plate over her missing bow for the long trip home.

Right : The *Bailey* (DD. 492), a *Bristol* Class destroyer, is seen here in December 1943. Her flat funnels distinguish her from the first group of *Bristol* Class destroyers.
Far right : The heavy cruiser *Minneapolis* (CA. 36) was torpedoed during the Battle of Tassafaronga, 30 November 1942. She is seen here in December, as work begins on cutting away her damaged bow.
Below : The transport *President Jackson* (AP. 37) turns under Japanese attack, 12 November 1942 off Guadalcanal. In the background is smoke from a Japanese plane which crashed into the *San Francisco* (CA. 38).

supply convoy. They commenced their attack shortly before noon and continued to maul Tanaka's Reinforcement Group for hours.

Prudence would have dictated that Tanaka retire to safer waters but to do so would have meant abandoning the effort to bring fresh troops and supplies to Guadalcanal. This Tanaka refused to do. Instead he ordered the eleven destroyers in his group to take on men and supplies from the ill-fated transports and proceed toward Guadalcanal. By that time at least seven transports had been lost and many men had died, this at the slight cost of five American planes shot down. The Tokyo Express had finally been stopped.

As American pilots returned from

their rout of Tanaka, another contest was brewing south of Savo Island between the dreadnoughts of Admiral Willis Lee and Nobutake Kondo. This battle, which took place on the night of 14–15 November, was one of the few of the Pacific War which pitted battlewagon against battlewagon. By the time the sun rose on 15 November Lee had prevailed and Admiral Kondo was in retreat. The United States had won yet another victory in the Naval Battle of Guadalcanal.

By 16 November 1942 the Battle for Guadalcanal was won. The United States had finally broken the stalemate that had prevailed since the beginning of August. It was several months before the Japanese withdrew entirely from Guadalcanal and Admiral Halsey could

Above: The *Fletcher* (DD. 445), one of the most famous destroyers of World War II, was the lead-ship of a new class of destroyers.
Far left: Scout and dive bombers on the forward deck of the *Enterprise* are refueled and rearmed after a raid on Marcus Island.

announce an American victory on 9 February 1943, but the tide had turned. Although the Americans ultimately claimed victory on Guadalcanal, it was a victory accomplished at tremendous cost in terms of life, limb and property. The Japanese, of course, paid an even greater price for their effort to hold the island. Guadalcanal will therefore always be remembered somberly.

Below: The *Thorn* (DD. 647) was one of the first group of the *Bristol* Class destroyers.

A convoy of transports crosses the Atlantic to take part in the invasion of North Africa, November 1942.

Operation Torch

Operation Torch was America's first venture in the European war. Although the North African campaigns were primarily an Army responsibility, the United States Navy played an important role in carrying tens of thousands of men and their equipment across the Atlantic in the largest amphibious operation in history until that date. Were it not for the tenacity and steel with which American and British naval officers carried out their part in the effort, it seems unlikely that the Axis powers would ever have been pushed out of North Africa.

The idea of Anglo-American landings in Morocco and Algeria was first discussed in December 1941, at which time Roosevelt and Churchill had concluded that the Allies would have to take some kind of initiative against the Axis in 1942, but it was not until several months later that the time and place of such an offensive was fixed. Initially, American military strategists favored a cross-Channel leap into France. The British, on the other hand, did not share the enthusiasm of their American allies *vis-a-vis* a return to France in 1942; 1943 seemed more realistic. In January 1942 both sides agreed to begin planning a Normandy landing for some time early in the spring of 1943. There remained, however, the matter of an offensive in 1942. Given the pressures exerted by the Soviets for a 'second front' to relieve their situation, some sort of action against Germany was absolutely necessary.

Following a series of conferences between American and Soviet leaders in early June 1942 President Roosevelt met with Prime Minister Churchill in Washington to discuss the matter of a second front. Coincidentally, as the two men were meeting, Rommel's forces took the British stronghold of Tobruk. If he was not stopped or diverted quickly it appeared likely that Rommel would soon enter Egypt. Now the idea of a second front was as critical to the Anglo-American Allies as to the Soviets and it would have to take place closer to Rommel's forces than the French coast.

By the end of July Anglo-American strategists came to the conclusion that landings in French Morocco and Algeria offered the only possible hope of thwarting the Axis offensive against the Suez lifeline. Such an offensive would also provide some relief to the Soviets. Accordingly, a planning staff was collected in London to prepare for the campaign. Within a few weeks the general outline of Operation Torch was ready for refinement.

Above left and right : Fighter pilots of Squadron 41 on board the USS *Ranger* (CV. 4). They are in the ready room waiting to take part in preliminary missions for Operation Torch. The pilots on the right, scheduled to take off before dawn, wear goggles to accustom their eyes to the dark.
Below : Red Beach at Fedala at 1100 hours, a few hours after the landings on 8 November 1942. This was Patton's main landing, executed by Center Task Group of Western Task Force, which met some opposition on the beaches but went on to take Casablanca.

The proposal for Operation Torch was fraught with all kinds of problems. It was unclear how the French would respond to Allied landings. If they chose to resist, then opposition could be formidable given the large number of French colonial forces in the area not to say anything of equally sizeable French naval forces in or close to these shores. Of equal importance was the logistical problem of safely ferrying large numbers of men and equipment across the Atlantic and through the Mediterranean. If Operation Torch was approved, it would be a risky venture.

The reservations of America and some British military and naval leaders notwithstanding, there was no viable alternative to the North African operation. Thus, a commitment to 'Torch' was made early in August and shortly thereafter General Eisenhower and Admiral Cunningham, RN, were appointed commanders of Allied Expeditionary Forces and Allied Naval Forces respectively. D-Day for the offensive was set for 30 October but later postponed until 8 November.

The final plan for Operation Torch was approved in September and called for the division of Anglo-American Forces into three separate task forces. The United States would have primary responsibility for the Eastern Task Force which was to capture Algiers. Responsibility for the Center Task Force, whose mission was to capture Oran, was to be shared, with the British supplying naval support and

As conceived by the planning group Operation Torch had four objectives. First, firm lodgements would be established between French Morocco and Tunisia. Once such bases were under Allied control, American and British forces would move east into Tunisia, attacking Axis forces from the rear. Caught between enemy forces on two sides, Rommel and his Italian allies would be forced to evacuate North Africa. If Operation Torch was successful, the Allies would have a stepping stone to Europe.

Left: Troops prepare for the main landings of the Western Task Force at Fedala on 8 November 1942 – successful, despite initial bad weather.

the United States the bulk of the combat troops. Overall coordination of these efforts rested with Eisenhower and Cunningham who remained behind in London.

The Western Task Force was commanded by Major General George Patton; the Western Naval Task Force by Rear Admiral H Kent Hewitt. Of the three units involved in Operation Torch, their mission was the most difficult for it involved carrying 35,000 men across 4500 miles of the Atlantic to strange beaches along the Moroccan coast. Many of the soldiers and sailors commanded by Patton and Hewitt had never seen action before and of those few who had, an even smaller number had any experience with amphibious operations.

There was little time available for training for Operation Torch and many hurdles to overcome, not the least of which was the matter of inter-service cooperation. In the history of the United States, there had never been a

Above : Sailors getting a few hours' sleep on board a transport off North Africa on the day before the Torch landings.

military effort which called for the kind of cooperation between the Army and Navy dictated by Operation Torch. Achieving such cooperation would be no easy matter given the personalities of the task force commanders, particularly Patton, and the difference in philosophies relative to amphibious operations that had been developed by the two services.

Since Hewitt and Patton operated independently of one another until their task force departed, each supervised his own preparations. Admiral Hewitt busied himself gathering transports and such landing craft as were available. While this was being done, intelligence relative to the area of the landings in French Morocco was culled from the other services, the State Department and civilians who had lived in the area with the assistance of those Marines who could be spared from Guadalcanal and the Pacific; naval personnel were drilled in techniques of amphibious warfare and engaged in simulated exercises off the American coast, while a special effort was made to find men experienced in small craft handling to maneuver the landing craft that would carry Patton's men ashore. Preparations were only partially complete when Task Force 34, as the combination of Patton's and Hewitt's forces was known, assembled to sail across the Atlantic on 23 October 1942.

The late Samuel E Morison once described Task Force 34 as 'a football team forced to play a major game very early in the season, before holding adequate practice or obtaining proper equipment.' This situation notwithstanding, Hewitt and Patton left for North Africa on 24 October determined to carry out their mission. If all went well, they would reach their destination by 7 November at which time Task Force 34 would divide into 3 operational units. A Center Attack Group was to land almost 20,000 troops at Fedala, 15 miles from Casablanca. A Northern Attack Group, 9000 strong, would land at Mehdia and seize the airport at Port Lyautey. A Southern Attack Group of 6500 was to land at Safi, 140 miles south of Casablanca, and bring ashore 125 tanks.

Given the uncertainty of French response to the American landings, secrecy was absolutely essential to the safety and success of the operation. Consequently, every precaution was taken to avoid tipping off potential adversaries. This was not an easy matter given the large size of the naval task force that would cross the Atlantic. In addition to the dozens of transports and support ships necessary to carry men and material to North Africa, there was a large naval support and air group which included a carrier and several battleships not to say anything of several cruisers and destroyer squadrons.

On 24 October 1942 troop transports and support vessels left Hampton Roads and were joined four days later by their Air Support Group which had embarked from Bermuda. In sum over 100 ships were involved in this operation which was unique in the annals of naval warfare. Never had such a large amphibious force been carried so far from their home ports for invasion of a strange continent. Such a mammoth undertaking was nothing less than fantastic but it was also quite dangerous given the presence of U-Boats in the Atlantic.

Task Force 34 proceeded without incident, refueling at sea on 31 October. It was not until 4 November that unusually rough seas and predictions of foul weather threatened the opera-

Above : A confident Patton goes ashore at Fedala. The army units had problems getting equipment from the beach to front line troops.

tion. If the weather did not clear and the seas calm, it would be difficult for the landing craft to be launched and the mission might have to be aborted. On the other hand, if Hewitt and Patton risked continuing the mission in the light of meteorological reports, the operation would commence but thousands might be lost unnecessarily.

Below : General Patton (left) and Admiral Hewitt (center) on the *Augusta* (CA. 31) as Patton prepares to go ashore on 9 November 1942.

Whatever course of action was chosen, it would be a risky one.

Based upon the educated guess of his staff meteorologist, Hewitt decided to go ahead with Torch. It proved to be the right decision for on 7 November the foul weather abated and the ocean swell moderated. By 1600 Hewitt's task force fractioned into three attack groups and moved toward the Moroccan coast. By 2400 all groups were in place and preparations were commenced for the first landings which were scheduled for 0400 on 8 November.

Of the three attack groups of Task Force 34, perhaps the most important was the Center Group which was to put ashore at Fedala near Casablanca. Center Group was composed of nearly 20,000 men, an almost equal number of naval support forces, and 1700 vehicles. Its mission was to capture Casablanca. The success or failure of Operation Torch would be decided by the fate of this mission.

Although there was an hour's delay in launching the first landing craft thanks to communication difficulties and inadequate training, Center Group was able to commence operations without detection or significant opposition from French authorities on the shore. Although some French officers had advance knowledge of an Allied landing they were generally favorably disposed to the Americans and British, but even had this not been the case it would not necessarily have mattered since precise details of the operation were never passed along to

Above : Sailors on the *Ranger* (CV. 4) strip the ship in anticipation of action off Morocco, early November 1942.

the French. It was not until later in the morning of 8 November that the presence of Task Force 34 was confirmed and even then the size of the Allied armada was not known. Thus, French resistance such as it was did not begin in earnest until after 0600, an hour after the landings began.

Despite some opposition from shore batteries and French naval vessels Center Group was able to carry out its assignment, although not without substantial losses of landing craft and personnel. By 1200 resistance ceased and clean-up work was initiated but it took considerably longer than expected to complete the landing of Patton's forces. Army men blamed the Navy for this delay; Navy personnel faulted the Army's amphibious landing philosophy. In truth, both services made their share of blunders; however, considering the fact that this was their first major cooperation venture of the war, all went comparatively well.

Simultaneous with the Fedala landing, the Southern Attack Group attacked Safi. They met with even less opposition than the Center Group. At 2345 on 7 November the first landing craft were lowered over the top of the transports, but it was not until after 0500 that they reached the beaches. As had been the case at Fedala, loading and launching the landing craft had taken longer than had been expected. Fortunately, once

Above: A 1.1-inch anti-aircraft gun crew closed up at battle stations aboard the carrier *Ranger* (CV.4) off North Africa in November 1942.
Left: The crew of a 1.1-inch anti-aircraft gun on the *Augusta* (CA. 31) taking a snack while closed up off North Africa in November 1942. Note the open breech of the gun on the left.

Left : A patrol craft fires a depth charge from a Y-gun while on duty chasing submarines off the North African coast in 1942.

again the element of surprise saved the Americans from potential losses. It was not until after the first raider party reached the shore that resistance began but this was quickly quashed thanks to aerial and fire support from the naval support force. Nevertheless, completion of the mission of the Southern Group took several days. It was not until 13 November that the unloading of tanks and men was completed. With Safi secured, French forces in Morocco were divided and the United States was able to bring heavy armored vehicles into North Africa.

The Northern Attack Group encountered more opposition than the Center and Southern Groups. As originally conceived, the mission of this force was to seize the airdrome at Port Lyautey, one of the only airstrips in North Africa with an all

Bottom : Crew remove the cork insulation as a fire precaution aboard the *Augusta*.

Above : Shells from the *Jean Bart* fall near a US warship off Casablanca. This was one of the rare occasions when the French Navy opposed Allied forces during the Torch landings on 8 November 1942.

Left : US TB destroyer escorts transports destined for North Africa.

Below : The fantail of the battleship *Massachusetts* (BB. 58) is seen during a lull in the action off Casablanca on 8 November 1942. She sank the French destroyers *Boulonnais* and *Fougueux* and damaged the battleship *Jean Bart*.

weather landing strip. Mehdia was to be the landing point for this effort. Over 9000 troops were to land there, the airport secured, and communication and transportation links between French Morocco and Algeria severed. Once again D-Day and H-Hour were set for 8 November at 0400.

The designation of Mehdia as a beachhead proved to be unfortunate in several respects. The port was more heavily fortified than others in the area, including Rabat, and the local French commander, General Mathenet, was far more hostile to the Allies than other French officers in Morocco. Given these circumstances, the Mehdia landing was a precarious affair which was further compromised by the fact that Mathenet had some advance warning of the presence of American forces and had put his forces on alert before American landing craft reached the shore.

As had been the case of Fedala and Safi, there was a considerable delay between the designated H-Hour and the actual time of the first landing at Mehdia which occurred about 0530. Within minutes after the first Americans landed ashore, the French opened fire from batteries on high ground near the Kasbah and just above the beach.

In addition, American forces were strafed by a handful of planes from the Rabat area. This combination of aerial and land bombardment continued for several hours before US naval forces were able to silence the shore batteries and chase the planes away. But this did not mark the end of the battle for French colonial forces refused to give way until the next day.

It was not until after nightfall on 9 November that American forces came within striking distance of the Port Lyautey airstrip and the Kasbah and even then, the landing operations were still incomplete. The next morning, however, circumstances changed for the better. The Kasbah was stormed and taken and at about the same time, ie 1030, the airfield was secured. With the fall of the Kasbah, resistance gradually came to an end and the landing of men and equipment was completed as American officers negotiated with French authorities for the passage of US forces to Rabat.

During the course of the first few days after D-Day for Operation Torch, the Navy played an important role in silencing shore batteries and chasing French vessels which attempted to harass and interrupt the landings. In this regard, such battlewagons as the New York and Texas were used successfully, proving the efficacy of employing their gunpower in support of an amphibious operation. If the aircraft carrier had eclipsed the dreadnought as the most important large naval weapon of World War II, the battleship still had an important role to play, albeit a far different one than in World War I.

Task Force 34, whose exploits have

been detailed above, was but one of three major task forces involved in Operation Torch. The other two were engaged in securing Algeria and were more exclusively British operations. Since the United States Navy played a relatively minor role in these missions, below is a brief survey of the events.

The landings at Algiers and Oran were beset by many of the same problems witnessed by American forces in Morocco, chief among them the unique nature of the venture and the scarcity of available equipment and adequately trained manpower. As in Morocco, the Allies encountered a mixed reception from French authorities in Algeria who suffered from the same confusion and mixed emotion as their colleagues to the West. What differed, however, was the presence of Axis forces in close proximity to the area and the willingness of Axis powers to commit some airpower

to thwart the Allied advance. Although such resistance did not prove critical in the end, it was an added nuisance and cost additional loss of life and limb.

By 15 November French resistance to the Anglo-American operations in North Africa had ceased. Admiral Darlan, the ranking French officer and colonial official in Algeria and Morocco, appointed General Henri Giraud as head of French forces in North Africa and Giraud, in turn, declared France's commitment to the defeat of Germany. This declaration climaxed the long and often bizarre diplomatic effort to bring the French into the fold and permitted the Allies to push into Tunisia where they hoped to catch Axis forces between British forces in Egypt and the Anglo-American forces in Morocco and Algeria.

During November and December 1942 additional manpower and sup-

Right : The flight deck of the *Chenango* (AO. 31/CVE. 28) and a destroyer crossing her wake are silhouetted against the darkening North African sky, November 1942.
Below : The destroyer *Schenck* (DD. 159) a *Wickes* Class destroyer was launched in 1919 but served the USN well in World War II.

plies were poured into North Africa, making it possible for Eisenhower to consider moving into Tunisia early in 1943. The Navy would continue to play an important support role during this new campaign, clearing North African ports of mines and debris, rendering them operable and patrolling the western Mediterranean. Once again, this support was vital to the success of US armed forces on land even if it was less dramatic and not often covered by the press.

The Tunisian campaign dragged on from January until May 1943. Unlike Algeria and Morocco where Anglo-American forces faced relatively weak and uncoordinated resistance from French forces and colonial troops, in Tunisia Allied forces faced a deter-mined and disciplined foe, brilliantly commanded by General Rommel. The Tunisian campaign was a sobering one for Allied leaders. It forced them to re-examine their plans for a cross-Channel invasion in 1943. By the time Tunisia fell into Allied hands it was clear that the next step to the European mainland would not be into France, but into Sicily.

Crewmen are briefed by an officer aboard the *Buck* (DD. 420) before the invasion of Sicily, on the ship's fantail. The *Buck* was sunk off Salerno on 9 October 1943.

Attacking the Boot

The successful completion of Operation Torch presented Allied leaders with the problem of what to do next. There was little opportunity or reason to gloat over Anglo-American victories in North Africa since the Germans and Japanese were still pressing hard against the US and the Soviets were holding on with all the tenacity they could bring to bear on Mother Russia, demanding some relief from the Western powers lest they succumb to the Nazi onslaught. It was under such conditions that Allied leaders assembled in Casablanca in January 1943 to plan their next move.

Discussions at Casablanca once again revealed serious differences between the American and British Joint Chiefs of Staff. As had been the case in earlier debates, the Americans pushed hard for a commitment to a cross-Channel move sometime in 1943 or early 1944. The British continued to resist such a move which they considered to be too risky given limited Allied capabilities and the ferocity and cunning with which German commanders had defended North Africa. If North Africa had been difficult, what would fortress Europe be like?

In place of a return to France the British suggested more modest proposals, including the possibility of a move from North Africa into Sardinia. With Sardinia secured, the Allies would have airfields within striking distance of northern Italy not to say anything of the capture of Maddalena Bay. British planners insisted that Sardinia could be taken in less than three months with minimal bloodletting, thus satisfying the continued Soviet demand for a Second Front without actually risking very much.

As might have been expected, American reaction to British proposals in general and the suggestion of a Sardinian campaign in particular was cool. However, when it became apparent that Churchill and his government were adamant in rejecting a cross-Channel venture, there was little choice but to consider some sort of invasion of Italian territory, but even then there were substantial differences of opinion between the two sides.

Admiral King reflected the views of his peers when he rejected the notion of invading Sardinia as 'doing something merely for the sake of doing something.' Instead, he suggested that Sicily be the next target of the Allies. Although it would be tougher to secure Sicily than Sardinia, it would give the Allies a stepping stone through which they could return to the European mainland. Furthermore, the fall of Sicily might be a sufficient political jolt to knock Mussolini off his 'throne.' To be sure, it would not be easy to take Sicily but it could be done and British objections notwithstanding it would be done and in the process the route to British colonies in the East would be insured and shortened.

After considerable discussion the Combined Chiefs of Staff designated

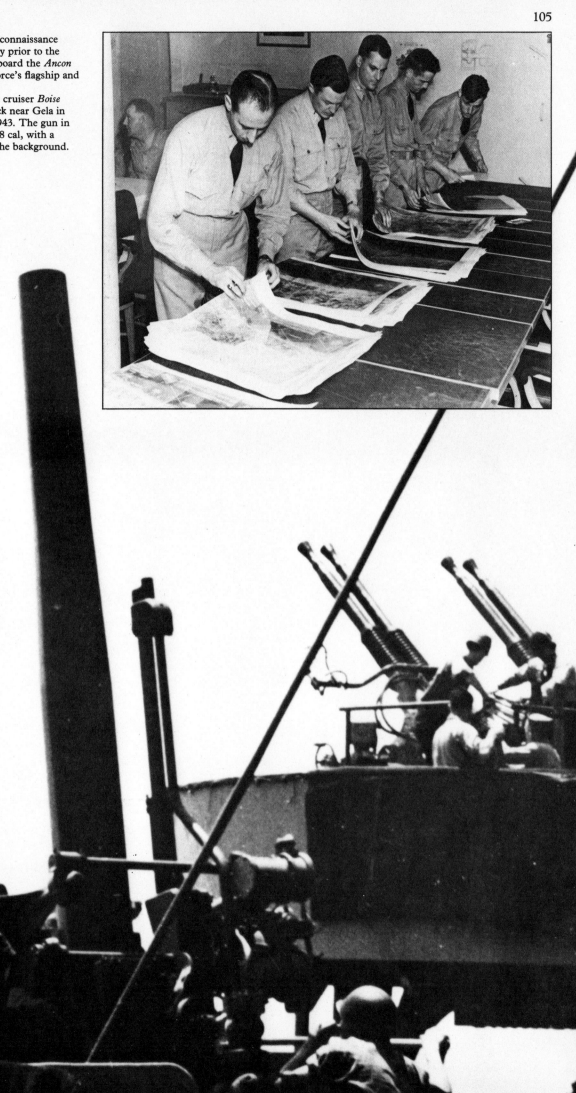

Right : Personnel examine reconnaissance photographs taken over Sicily prior to the landings on 2 July 1943, on board the *Ancon* (AGC. 4), the amphibious force's flagship and temporary headquarters.

Below : Gunners on the light cruiser *Boise* (CL. 47) fight off an air attack near Gela in southern Sicily on 10 July 1943. The gun in the foreground is a 5-inch/.38 cal, with a quadruple 40mm Bofors in the background.

Above: General Mark Clark (left) and Rear Admiral Alan Kirk on the *Ancon* (AGC. 4).
Right top: Following the Sicily campaign, the US Navy prepared for the landings in Italy. LCVPs (Landing Craft Vehicles, Personnel) head for Salerno, 9 September 1943.
Right center: DUKWs (amphibious trucks) are unloaded from a LST at Red Beach, Salerno, with a Bofors gun in the foreground.
Below: Troops from the *James O'Hara* (APA. 90) were attacked at Salerno. Chicken wire stabilizes the sandy beach.

the conquest of Sicily as their next goal on 19 January 1943. Three days later a scenario for Operation Husky was ready for the participants at the Casablanca Conference. They endorsed the proposal before the Conference adjourned the next day with a tentative D-Day set for mid-summer of 1943. This done, it was necessary to establish a command for the new venture.

In selecting a commander for Operation Husky, Allied leaders naturally looked favorably upon retaining the winning team behind Operation Torch, namely General Eisenhower and Admiral Cunningham, RN. Despite some problems of protocol posed by Eisenhower's relatively junior status *vis-à-vis* his British counterparts, Churchill and Roosevelt

worked their will and on 23 January Eisenhower and Cunningham were informed of their appointments as overlords of Operation Husky.

Within weeks after receiving their charge Eisenhower and Cunningham assembled a staff for the Sicilian campaign. With some minor exceptions it was to be the same group which had successfully executed the North African offensive, including Vice-Admiral H Kent Hewitt who had so ably commanded the Western Task Force during Operation Torch.

On 10 February General Eisenhower established a planning staff for Operation Husky. Shortly thereafter Admiral Cunningham followed suit. Although these two groups eventually joined forces in Algiers, Air Force planning, under the command of Air Marshal Tedder, was not coordinated with that of the other services, a fact that was to have unfortunate consequences at a later day. Planning for Operation Husky continued for several months but by the middle of March a rough plan was presented to Cunningham and Eisenhower.

The initial plan for Operation Husky called for the seizure of Catania and Palermo by nine divisions of Allied Forces to be landed at two widely separated beachheads in southern Sicily. The ultimate goal of the offensive, once these ports were secured, was to isolate Sicily by capturing Messina, but before this could be accomplished Allied forces would have to gain mastery of the skies over the island and insure that the formidable Italian Fleet did not interfere with the initial landings.

Reaction to the initial plan was mixed. The British in particular ob-

jected to the distance between the two task forces and the sites chosen for the landings, which lacked harbors adequate to handle problems of supply once the operation was underway. They suggested instead that the initial targets of the assault be redefined, with Palermo being dropped from the list of sites under consideration. After much soul searching, Eisenhower and Cunningham agreed to revise the initial draft so as to create a more limited thrust in southern and eastern Sicily. Even then the undertaking was a mammoth one, dwarfing the amphibious operations of the North African campaign.

The revised plan called for the division of Allied resources into two task forces. A Western Task Force under the command of Admiral Hewitt was to land between Licata and Scoglitti. An Eastern Task Force under the command of Admiral Ramsay, RN, was to land on the Pachino Peninsula near Syracuse about fifty miles to the east of the Western Task Force. In total, eight divisions were to be landed on D-Day which was now set for 10 July.

Admiral Hewitt, who was responsible for ferrying the Seventh Army under the command of George Patton to Sicily, divided his Task Force into three attack groups under the commands of Rear Admiral R L Conolly, Rear Admiral J L Hall and Rear Admiral Alan Kirk respectively. Conolly's group (Joss Force) would land near Licata. Hall's group (Dime Force) would land at Gela. Kirk's group (Cent Force) would land at Scoglitti. To the east or right flank of Kirk, the Eastern Task Force would be landing General Montgomery's army.

To accomplish his goals, Admiral Hewitt had a task force in excess of 550 vessels and 1100 landing craft. To move such an armada safely posed many problems, particularly in light of the poor beaches in southern Sicily and the potential strength of the enemy. Unlike North Africa where the Allies faced relatively weak and frequently vacillating French forces, in Sicily they faced more serious opposition which included the Royal Italian Navy. This necessitated special efforts to confuse the enemy as to the where-

Right : Crews fight a fire in No 3 6-inch turret aboard the light cruiser *Savannah* (CL. 42) following a bomb hit from a German glider-bomb off Salerno, Italy. This was a later operation, September 1943, undertaken by the US Navy.
Far right : Ensign T E Jameson is returned to the *Santee* (CVE. 29) on 29 July 1943. The *Santee* was returning to the USA after a tour of duty in the Mediterranean.
Below : Coast guards and Navy beach battalions hug the beach south of Salerno, during the main landings in Italy, September 1943.

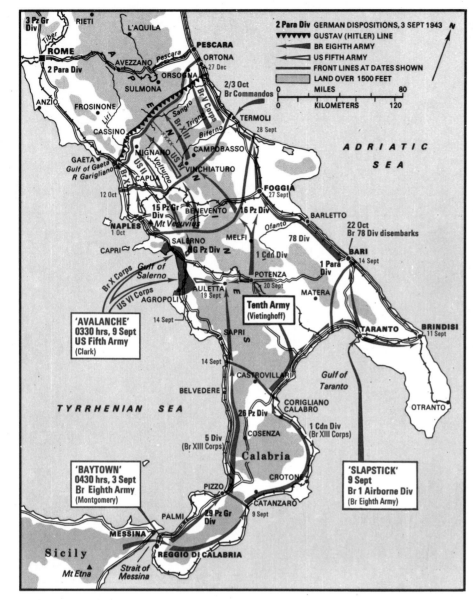

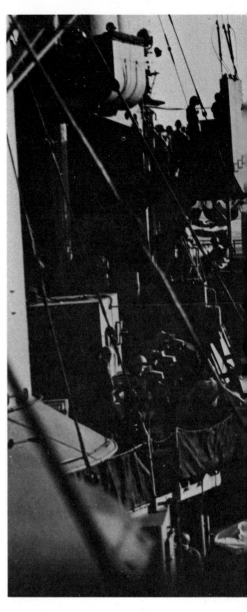

abouts of an attack and should have required Anglo-American aerial units to provide superior coverage and protection. The former problem was resolved by the use of an elaborate intelligence hoax and plant designed to convince German and Italian leaders that Greece was the real target of the next Allied attack. The problem of air support was never successfully resolved.

For almost two months the Allied Task Forces prepared for the invasion of Sicily. On 8 July they embarked upon the relatively short journey from North Africa to Sicily. As had been the case during Operation Torch, the weather worsened as Allied forces prepared to commence their mission. Indeed there was even some thought given to delaying departure but this idea was dismissed, based upon the fear that delay might jeopardize the 'surprise element' of the attack. Fortunately the weather cleared sufficiently to permit landings without incident. More important, Italian and German forces on Sicily seemed to be taken in by the intelligence hoax

mentioned previously and despite the fact that some Axis military leaders suspected the imminence of a landing in Sicily, little was actually done to prepare for it. Thus, if Operation Husky was not a total surprise to Axis forces, it caught them sufficiently off guard to allow for the successful execution of the first phase of the mission.

By 0100 on 10 July the three attack groups of the Western Naval Task Force had reached their respective launching positions off the Sicilian coast. At approximately 0410 the first landing craft from Joss Force were sent ashore, reaching their destination by 0435. By that time Dime Force had already completed the first phase of its landing operations while Cent Force was in midst of securing beaches near Scoglitti.

Of the three attack groups Joss Force had the easiest time of it. The beaches near Licata where this group landed were almost ideal for an amphibious operation. Furthermore, Italian forces in the vicinity were caught almost totally off guard by the

landings which occurred under the cover of early morning darkness. American forces were therefore able to claim complete control of the village of Licata before noon. The Joss landing was an almost perfect opera-operation. Unfortunately the other two attack groups did not fare so well.

Dime Force encountered unusually stiff opposition in its efforts to secure the Gela area. The beachheads near Gela were poor by comparison to those adjacent to Licata and they were more heavily fortified. It took paratroops over four hours to silence and seize the batteries in Gela and even after the village was taken resistance continued as German and Italian aircraft bombed and strafed American forces. In its efforts to secure the beachheads and cope with Axis attackers, Dime Force received virtually no help from the RAF or Army Air Force units, nor did its peers to the west and east fare any better in this regard. Considering the congestion of equipment and men on the beaches near Gela and the proximity of Italian forces in the area this absence of air support could have

Above : A destroyer is one of the many vessels
'making smoke' during a red alert at Salerno,
Italy.
Right : Secretary of Navy, Frank Knox, on an
inspection tour of Italy in October 1943,
confers with General Patton and Vice-Admiral
Kent Hewitt.

proved fatal to the mission of Dime
Force. Fortunately, that was not to be
the case.

Given the absence of air support it
fell upon the Navy to knock out Axis
batteries and tanks in the vicinity of
Gela. As had been the case in North
Africa, spotters on shore were able to
pinpoint enemy emplacements and
radio these positions back to the
destroyers and cruisers of the support
fleet whose batteries were then used
effectively to silence the enemy. Were
it not for this naval artillery support
the Gela landings might have been
aborted. As it was it took four days
before it could be said that the area
was secure.

Cent Force, which was responsible
for securing Scoglitti and neutralizing
Italian air bases at Biscari and Comiso,
had the most important mission of the

Above : A destroyer lays down a smokescreen during a German air raid. The photograph was taken from the *Ancon.*
Far right : Secretary of Navy, James Forrestal and Admiral Kent Hewitt inspect a new beachhead after D-Day, 15 August 1943.

three groups of the Western Task Force and with 26,000 troops to be landed was the largest of them all. Fortunately, opposition to these landings on two beaches some seven miles apart was minimal. The problem for Admiral Kirk was not one of silencing Axis batteries and tanks on shore or evading enemy aircraft. Rather, it was one of the inadequacy of the beaches chosen for the landings to handle the large amount of equipment and numbers of men to be put ashore. Many landing craft went aground, while others waited patiently for the chance to unload their cargoes. The pile-up could have presented the enemy with an easy target had there been more than a half-hearted effort by Axis forces in the vicinity of Scoglitti to contest the landings. Fortunately, that was not the case except for an encounter between the 180th Regiment and units of the Hermann Goering Division.

The Eastern Naval Task Force, under the command of Admiral Bertram Ramsay, encountered the same problems as Hewitt's Western Task Force: inadequate beaches, congestion and pile-ups and occasional enemy resistance. Like their American counterparts, the British successfully solved these problems and by 16 July were firmly in control of their beachheads and ready to proceed to Phase II of Operation Husky, the race toward Messina.

With the successful conclusion of the Western and Eastern Naval Task Forces, the responsibility for seizing and securing Sicily fell to the United States and British armies respectively. The US Navy and Royal Navy played only a secondary role between 15 July and 17 August when Sicily was overrun. Nevertheless, without the continued support of naval artillery, intelligence and mine sweeping operations it is doubtful whether Allied forces could have moved as rapidly as they did.

The successful conquest of Sicily was to have more profound consequences than Allied leaders had ever imagined, not all of which were to prove advantageous. The relative ease with which Allied forces captured Augusta, Gela, Licata, Scoglitti and Syracuse forced Mussolini to seek immediate relief from Hitler. It also weakened his political stature sufficiently to permit King Victor Emmanuel III to replace Mussolini with Marshal Badoglio and to put Il Duce under house arrest. Although the Badoglio regime quickly reconfirmed its loyalty to the Axis it became clear to the Germans that if Italy was to be held they would have to do the holding. There could be no further reliance on the 'Italian connection.' To the misfortune of the Allies Hitler, not Mussolini, would now be their primary opponent in Italy.

Below : The light cruiser *Brooklyn* (CL. 40)
supported the US landings in Sicily and Italy.
The *Brooklyn* Class was built after 1935 and
inspired by the Japanese *Mogami* Class.

Troops unload ammunition from LCTs
(Landing Craft, Tank) at Rendova Island
New Georgia in June 1943.

Across the Pacific

The victory on Guadalcanal in February 1943 marked the conclusion of the first phase of Operation Watchtower, the object of which was to break through the Bismarck Barrier as a prelude to a return to the Philippines and the ultimate defeat of Japan. Once this victory was won, American leaders had to determine whether to proceed with the plan favored by General MacArthur and his staff, which called for concentration of all US military and naval forces under his control in a massive effort along the axis stretching from New Guinea to the Philippines, or another scheme proposed by the Navy which suggested a second route to Japan across the Central Pacific to be carved out simultaneously with MacArthur's redemption of his promise to return to the Philippines.

Given the strong personalities and opinions of senior commanders in the Pacific it was no easy matter for the Joint Chiefs of Staff to resolve the differences between Army and Navy men. It was several months after the Japanese evacuated Guadalcanal before final decisions on strategy were made and even then there was considerable disagreement on them. In

Top left : The *Worden* (DD. 352) sinks off Amchitka in the Aleutians, 12 January 1943. The *Dewey* (DD. 349) stands by.
Above : The *Wickes* (DD. 578), a member of the *Fletcher* Class, heads out to open sea in January 1943.
Left : The *Bagley* (DD. 386) was a member of the *Gridley* Class and had 16 torpedo tubes. She is seen here prewar.
Below : The *Chicago* (CA. 29) is photographed from the *Wichita* (CA. 45) with the *Louisville* (CA. 28) in the background, prior to the Battle of Russell Island of 29 January 1943. The next 'hop' took them to New Georgia.

Above: The powerful fleet destroyer *Blue* (DD. 744) of the *Allen M Sumner* Class incorporated standard twin 5-inch/38 cal turrets on the basic *Fletcher* hull, but had a broader beam.

the end, however, all hands joined together and 1943 witnessed yet more progress against Japan.

In determining how to proceed after Guadalcanal, American military planners were greatly influenced by the Guadalcanal campaign which had proven beyond a doubt how difficult it would be to oust the Japanese from those areas where they were present in force and determined to hold. If Guadalcanal was any indication of what American forces had to contend with, it would be many years before the Allies drew near Japan and the cost in men and equipment would be huge. Considering the priority given to operations in North Africa, Sicily and Italy, it would be difficult if not impossible for the United States to meet the needs of such a war of attrition in the Pacific. As a consequence, the Joint Chiefs eventually decided to allow Nimitz and the Navy the chance to open a second route to Japan through the Gilbert and

Below: Coastal patrol craft *PC. 551* drops a depth charge.

Marshall Islands, in the hope that such a campaign would be able to break the back of Japanese resistance at a lesser cost than MacArthur's original proposals.

While the question of what to do next was still being debated, it was necessary to clear the Solomon Islands of Japanese resistance before launching phase two of Operation Watchtower. As long as the Japanese were in a position to harass Allied forces on Guadalcanal, Tulagi and elsewhere in the Solomons, it would be difficult to mount the next major campaigns. Consequently, the Joint Chiefs ordered Nimitz and MacArthur to neutralize the Solomons and establish bases on New Britain as a prerequisite for continued progress in the Pacific. It was hoped that the campaign could be completed by the early summer.

Of the Japanese strongholds in the Solomons none was more important than their air base at Munda from which American installations were regularly attacked. Not unnaturally, this became the prime target of the American effort to secure the Solomons. At the end of June a large amphibious force under the command

of Rear Admiral Kelly Turner was assembled near Guadalcanal for the purpose of ferrying American forces to Munda, where they would engage the enemy in an effort to seize the airfield and capture the island.

Several thousand American troops were landed on New Georgia during the first days of July. From the moment of their first landing, the Americans encountered stiff resistance from the Japanese who attempted to bolster their own strength by running the now infamous Tokyo Express down the Slot yet once more. Unlike the situation that had prevailed during the Guadalcanal campaign when the Imperial Navy was able to ferry its troops back and forth with little or no contest, Nimitz and his lieutenants were much more aggressive in engaging night-running convoys, actively seek-

Top center : Patrol boat *No 39* (ex-destroyer *Tade*), was sunk by the submarine *Seawolf* (SS. 197) on 23 April 1943.
Top right : Marine PBJ bombers out on a raid on Rabaul in mid-1943.
Above : The first Americans ashore at Rendova take cover in dawn landings in heavy rain on New Georgia, June 1943.

The destroyer *Stevens* (DD. 479) experimented with a catapult and floatplane in 1943 to provide reconnaissance, but carrier aircraft and radar were more efficient.

The new destroyer escort *Levy* (DE. 162) runs trials in May 1943. Designed for the Atlantic these *Cannon* Class and other DEs also served in the Pacific.

ing the enemy out. As a consequence, there were several significant clashes between the two Navies paralleling the battle on land.

The United States Navy enjoyed numerical superiority over the Imperial Navy in the encounters that took place around New Georgia but the Japanese proved to be remarkably tough adversaries. While Japanese ships lacked radar they were equipped with radar detectors which permitted them to fix the whereabouts of the Americans, often before the US could get a fix on them. Of greater signific-

ance perhaps was the fact that Japanese torpedo technology was still well in advance of American, allowing them much greater range and accuracy. Nevertheless, irrespective of their technical superiority or skill at moving men and equipment into and out of Munda, attrition took a heavy toll on the Japanese which they could ill afford.

The stubbornness of Japanese resistance is well illustrated by the fact that it took over 30,000 American forces nearly two months to seize New Georgia from a Japanese garrison of only one-quarter that size. It was not until 5 August that the Stars and Stripes was raised over the air base at Munda and even then the Japanese

Navy continued to be a nuisance, although increasingly more aggressive tactics by American naval commanders would eventually neutralize the threat to the Solomons.

The difficulties which American forces encountered in trying to capture Munda provided yet another indication to the Joint Chiefs that if a systematic linear island-to-island progression was to be continued, it would

Patrol Torpedo Boats (PTs) ferry troops ashore and cover landings in Nassau Bay, New Guinea, 6 July 1943.

Oily survivors of the light cruiser *Helena* (CL. 50) which had been hit by three torpedoes board the *Nicholas* (DD. 449).

take years if not decades before Japan was subdued. Clearly, a new strategy was in order. Island-hopping was unsatisfactory. But what was the alternative? The answer was found to be leapfrogging.

Until August 1943 American forces had chosen to engage the Japanese where they were well ensconced. Indeed, one of the primary goals of Operation Watchtower remained the capture of Rabaul, Japan's major base in the southwest Pacific. By the end of the Munda campaign, Allied leaders began to re-examine the wisdom of this approach. If Guadalcanal and

other encounters in the Solomons had proved so costly, what might one expect to happen at Rabaul? Although no one was ready to publicly advocate by-passing Rabaul, privately many gave this idea serious consideration, including the Joint Chiefs of Staff.

By the time of the Quebec Conference (August 1943), Allied military leaders had come to the conclusion that it was no longer feasible or necessary to seize Rabaul. They proposed, instead, to isolate Rabaul by leapfrogging around it and leaving air power based on both sides of this enemy stronghold to pulverize it. Rather than push on to Rabaul, Allied forces would now push on to the Admiralties, Gilberts and Marshalls

The light minelayer *Pruitt* (DM. 22) escorts landing boats from the transport *Heywood* (AP. 12) to the beach on Massacre Bay, Attu, Aleutian Islands, 11 May 1943.

but before this took place there would be one last major campaign to drive the Japanese out of the Solomons – Bougainville.

Bougainville was attractive to the Joint Chiefs because it was near enough to Rabaul to be developed as a base for fighter aircraft which lacked the range of larger craft now partially based at Munda. Since the island was

Below: The destroyer *Halford* (DD. 480) is seen on trials in July 1943. The catapult and floatplane were removed after the trials.
Bottom: The *Fletcher* Class destroyer *Cony* (DD. 508) 'at ease' in the South Pacific.

The destroyer *Conway* (DD. 507) escorted one of the convoys which supplied troops in the southwest Pacific. Convoys were under perpetual risk of attack.

relatively large, it would be possible to land American forces on one end sufficiently distant from the main Japanese garrison on the island to permit them to dig in and open airstrips before the enemy could counterattack.

At the end of October 1943 Empress Augusta Bay was designated as the site of the Allied landing on Bougainville and an amphibious force of almost 15,000 men and a dozen transports, plus support craft under the command of Rear Admiral Theodore Wilkinson and Lieutenant General A A Vandegrift, was gathered for the assault. D-Day was 1 November.

Empress Augusta Bay had been selected for Allied landings because intelligence revealed few enemy troops in the area. This estimate proved

Lieutenant Commander Ernest Evans, her commanding officer, performs the commissioning ceremonies for the *Johnston* (DD. 557) on 27 October 1943. She died heroically in the Battle of Leyte Gulf in October 1944.

correct. When the first waves of American forces landed they encountered almost no resistance save for Japanese air attacks from Rabaul and an effort by the Imperial Navy to break up the landings, both of which failed; the former thanks to air cover provided by the Army Air Force from bases elsewhere in the Solomons and the latter thanks to the lessons learned by the Navy from the many battles adjacent to Guadalcanal.

In the Bougainville campaign, the Navy played considerably more than a support role. In addition to ferrying men and supplies to Empress Augusta Bay, the Navy provided air power launched from the carriers *Saratoga*, *Princeton*, *Essex*, *Independence* and *Bunker Hill* which attacked Japanese installations at Rabaul and Truk and engaged a Japanese naval task force which had been dispatched to Bougainville. The toll of these aggressive attacks was heavy. Although Rabaul was not completely decimated, scores of enemy aircraft were destroyed on the ground.

Despite the crippling blows struck against Rabaul by American naval air power, Bougainville was not easily

secured. The Japanese garrison of 60,000 was able to hold on to the island for nearly four months. However, in their efforts to wipe out American strongholds the Japanese sustained heavy losses, which allowed somewhat numerically inferior Allied forces to obtain victory in March 1944.

As the Battle for Bougainville entered its last phase, American forces under the command of General MacArthur were landed on the Admiralty Islands. With the assistance of the 7th Fleet, they succeeded in defeating an enemy force of almost 5000 men by the beginning of April 1944. The seizure of the Admiralties provided the Allies with yet another base within striking distance of Rabaul and a fine harbor from which to stage new campaigns which would lead back to the Philippines and Japan.

Although the Navy was very much involved in operations in the Admiralties and Bougainville, much of the time and energy of Nimitz and his staff was given to the planning of operations in the Gilbert and Marshall Islands. As mentioned earlier in this chapter, the Joint Chiefs had given their blessings to these operations in the hope that capture of bases in the Western Pacific would put the Allies in a position from which they could launch aerial assaults on the Japanese home islands. The path to the Western Pacific cut through Micronesia, hence the importance of the Gilberts and Marshalls.

Operation Galvanic, as the Micronesian campaign was coded, was to take place simultaneously with MacArthur's push into New Guinea. The first targets of this operation were to be Makin and Tarawa which would be converted into air bases for the latter part of the offensive in the Marshalls and Carolines. D-Day for the first round of Galvanic was set for November. The 5th Fleet under the command of Vice-Admiral Spruance, a seasoned veteran of the Pacific War, was to carry out the mission with Kelly Turner assigned to assist Spruance in coordinating the amphibious part of the operation.

Above : The escort *Acree* (DE. 167) of the
Cannon Class makes her way to the Pacific
in 1943.
Above right : Another member of the *Fletcher*
Class, the *McCord* (DD. 534) lies at anchor.
Right : In full camouflage, the destroyer escort
Naifeh (DE. 352) six months after she was
launched. She was a *John C Butler* Class DE.
Below : The *Selfridge* (DD. 357) was badly
damaged in the Battle of Vella Lavella in
October 1943. The wrecked No 2 5-inch gun
mount is all that is left of the bow after a hit
from a Japanese 'Long Lance' torpedo.

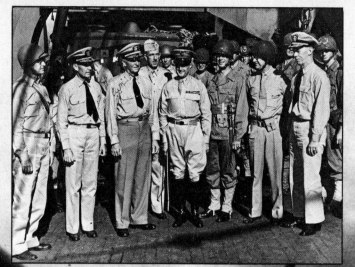

Top left : The veteran battleship *Colorado*
(BB. 45) bombards Tarawa with her after
16-inch turrets in November 1943.
Top right : Corpses line the beaches at Tarawa
after the Marines landed. Despite heavy losses,
5000 men landed on Tarawa on the first day of
battle.
Above right : The directors of Central Pacific
Operations: left to right – Rear Admiral
R Kelly Turner, Vice-Admiral Raymond
Spruance, Admiral Nimitz, Brigadier General
Holmes, Lieutenant General R C Richardson,
Major General Ralph Smith, Major General
H 'Howling Mad' Smith and Rear Admiral
C H Morris.
Right : A Grumman F6F Hellcat bursts into
flames while landing on the *Enterprise* (CV. 6)
during the Gilbert Islands campaign.

During the interim from July-November, intelligence teams accumulated what information was available on Tarawa and Makin and supplemented it with aerial reconnaissance. As D-Day drew near, air strikes were launched to destroy what installations of military significance were known to be on these atolls. Since intelligence revealed limited Japanese strength on both islands, it was thought that they would be seized with minimal difficulty. Such was not to be the case, at least insofar as Tarawa was concerned.

Makin was relatively easily secured thanks to the vast numerical superiority of American forces. However, the victory was not achieved without cost. Japanese submarines penetrated Turner's naval defenses and torpedoed a transport. In addition several night raids were carried out against the 5th Fleet, costing additional losses and damage but not enough to prevent the capture of Makin by 26 November.

As the Makin landing force was completing operations on that atoll an even larger force was landed on Tarawa on 20 November. For several hours before H-Hour carrier based aircraft ran dozens of missions over the island, but when the first Americans waded ashore they soon discovered the enemy was barely shaken from his defensive positions by these attacks. Thousands of Marines were pinned down on the beach and a large amount of equipment and supplies was lost, including many landing craft.

Despite sustaining very heavy losses, 5000 men were landed on Tarawa by the end of the first day of the battle. Over the next few days, American forces succeeded in breaking the back of Japanese resistance. By 23 November Tarawa was in American hands. There was not much cause for jubilation over the victory at Tarawa. Over 1000 men lost their lives and hundreds more were hurt or wounded during this three-day battle. Once again, the Japanese had proved to be worthy foes and obstinate enemies.

With the Gilbert Islands secured, Nimitz and his staff prepared for a thrust into the Marshall Islands thus initiating Phase II of Operation Galvanic. Of the many possible targets for such an assault, Kwajalein was chosen as the focus of the operation with Majuro and Eniwetok designated as secondary but still important targets. Kwajalein was so designated because it was fast developing into Japan's major defense center in the Marshalls and contained installations which posed a serious threat to the continued progress of the Allied war effort. Normally, Kwajalein might have been leapfrogged for the very same reasons that made it a likely target, but thanks to newly acquired airstrips on Makin and Tarawa it was feasible to engage the Japanese at the center of their strength.

The landing on Kwajalein was a major undertaking in view of the atoll's large size and the presence of sizeable numbers of enemy forces. As conceived by Vice-Admiral Kelly Turner, Commander of the Expeditionary Force, the Kwajalein campaign would be a two-pronged attack with Allied forces divided into Northern and Southern Attack Groups. The Northern Group was to take Roi and Namur and the Southern Group to take Kwajalein itself. D-Day for the attack was set for 31 January 1944.

As a result of sad experience on Tarawa, efforts to soften enemy resistance through attack commenced at least three days before D-Day and continued through the morning of

Above : Admiral Kelly Turner at the
Kwajalein Landings.
Above left : Marines dash ashore during the
invasion of Tarawa in the Gilbert Islands,
November 1943.
Left : The .50 cal water-cooled AA machine
gun was replaced after 1942 by the heavier
and more effective 20mm Oerlikon gun, but
was still fitted on the older carriers in the early
part of the Central Pacific campaign.
Above right : Admiral Nimitz (CINCPAC) with
chart and Vice-Admiral Spruance
(ommander of the 5th Fleet) in the center,
tour Kwajalein Island in the Marshalls on
5 February 1944.
Below : A Nakajima B5N 'Kate' is shot down
during an attack on a US carrier during a US
Navy raid on the Marshalls, December 1944.

Above : The destroyer *Melvin* (DD. 680) of the *Fletcher* Class on trials in December 1943.
Left : The *Essex* Class aircraft carrier *Intrepid* (CV. 11) makes way in the Pacific in January 1944. She and her sister ships of the *Essex* Class had more than adequate speed and aircraft capacity, and became the new capital ships of the Pacific War.

31 January when both task forces reached their destinations. Because of less than favorable beaching conditions that prevailed at the designated places of attack, there was confusion and delay in putting men and their supplies ashore. This was exacerbated by Japanese resisters who were supported by raiding bombers launched from Ponape.

In spite of the obstacles they had to overcome, Allied forces successfully carved out beachheads in the north and south by the end of the day on 1 February. For the next week they engaged the Japanese regularly, battling the enemy for every yard of territory gained. By 8 February the atoll had been secured by the 40,000 men who had been landed. In defending this stronghold the Japanese had literally fought to the last man, sacrificing 8000 men out of a garrison of 8500 in the process.

Having secured Kwajalein, American forces leapfrogged over the rest of the Marshall Islands, choosing the westernmost of this group, Eniwetok, as their next target. Before launching this attack, a special effort was made to neutralize Japanese air power on Ponape and Truk. By the time that D-Day 17 February, arrived for the Eniwetok operation, these Japanese bases had been severely damaged so that when American forces landed on Eniwetok Atoll they were not harassed by enemy aircraft. Nevertheless Eniwetok was not an easy operation.

There were considerably more Japanese defenders on Eniwetok than American or Allied intelligence had led theater commanders to believe and like their peers elsewhere in the Pacific, Japanese forces in the atoll were also willing to fight to the death before surrendering any territory. Thus, what should have taken only two or three days to accomplish actually took almost a week. It was not until 23 February that Eniwetok was cleared of the enemy.

Eniwetok concluded the Allied offensive in the Marshalls. Having seriously breached Japan's outer defense perimeter sights were now set on the Marianas which, if taken, would provide the Allies with bases within bombing distance of the enemy's homeland.

Bottom left : The submarine *Tinosa* (SS. 283) returns from a war patrol in 1944 to her base at Pearl Harbor.
Bottom center : Warships engaged in surface operations northwest of Truk Island in the Carolines as seen from the deck of the *Iowa* (BB. 61), 16 February 1944.
Below : The destroyer escort *Tatum* (DE. 789) approaches cruising speed in the Pacific, 1944.

Crewmen prepare US Navy Curtiss SB2C Helldiver dive bombers for takeoff. Note that life rafts are being placed in the 'ready' position immediately below a battery of 20mm machine guns ranged along the edge of the carrier's flight deck.

The Momentum Gathers

With Kwajalein and Eniwetok safe in hand, the Navy was ready to commence an attack on the Marianas. Operation Forager, as this campaign was coded, had three immediate objectives: seizure of Saipan, Tinian and Guam. Possession of these islands and the air bases the Japanese had constructed on them would put the Allies in a position adjacent to the Bonin Islands and within reasonably close striking distance of Okinawa and Japan. Needless to say, Allied military leaders understood only too well that the Japanese would not yield their territory without a terrific fight. If they had waged suicidal resistance in trying to preserve Japan's outer defenses, how much blood would be let protecting the inner defenses of the Empire?

The nature of the forthcoming campaign in the Marianas dictated the collection of the largest amphibious force of the Pacific War to that date and the assignment of appropriately large support groups to the operation. Fortunately, the Navy had never been in a better position to meet the needs of such a major offensive nor had American air power ever been so overwhelming. In short, Operation Forager would not want for men, equipment and supplies, or adequate naval and aerial assault material.

Overall responsibility for Operation Forager was divided between Admirals Spruance and Turner. Turner, by now an 'expert' in the art of island-hopping and leapfrogging, would be in charge of amphibious operations. Spruance would be responsible for coordinating support forces and working out logistical problems of supplying Allied forces of over 125,000 men who were to be landed on Saipan, the first target of the campaign, in mid-July 1944. Spruance's staff was also to be responsible for base development after the Marianas were secured, also no mean feat.

The sheer size of Operation Forager boggled the mind. To transport over 125,000 men 1000 and more miles required the services of hundreds of vessels. To satisfy these needs, carrier forces which had hitherto operated under Admiral Halsey's command were diverted from the southwest Pacific and attached to Spruance's command. In addition all available submarines of the Pacific Fleet were sent to Eniwetok. By the time the Forager Task Force left for Saipan it was composed of almost 600 ships, including fifteen aircraft carriers, seven battleships, 22 cruisers and 69 destroyers – a considerable armada!

Experience had shown the import-

Above: Admirals Spruance (left), Nimitz and Sherman (back to camera) aboard the battleship *New Jersey* (BB. 62) off the Marshalls in April 1944.
Right above: A Japanese coaster is strafed by aircraft belonging to Squadron 106 in the Southwestern Pacific in 1944.
Right center: Aerial view of Japanese ships taking evasive action following an air attack during the Battle of the Philippine sea in June 1944.

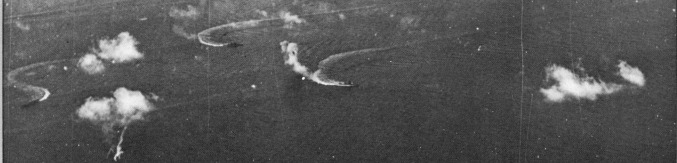

Below : Republic P-47s on the deck of the escort carrier *Manila Bay* (CVE. 61) during an attack by four Japanese planes from Saipan Island. The aircraft are being ferried out to the Pacific Theater as deck-cargo.

Above: The Combined Chiefs of Staff decided on the Central Pacific advance only after considerable pressure from Admirals King and Nimitz.

Above: Admiral Marc Mitscher.
Right: The battleship *New Mexico* (BB. 40) fires her guns in support of the Saipan landings in June 1944. Note that the center 14-inch gun has recoiled.

ance of softening enemy defenses before attempting any large-scale amphibious operation. Accordingly, regular strikes were commenced against Japanese installations in the Marianas in mid-May, a full month before D-Day for the Saipan landing, and these raids were continued on a regular basis thereafter. In addition to using carrier based aircraft for such attacks, battleship artillery barrages were also employed. No stone was left

Below: Admiral Spruance (left) was the commander for the Marianas operation and Major General Holland Smith led the V Amphibious Corps on Saipan.

unturned to spare American forces from the blood letting that had occurred on the beaches of Tarawa. Thus, submarines were also usefully deployed to prevent the Japanese from supplying their garrison of 25,000 plus on Saipan and from reinforcing it.

D-Day for the Saipan landing was 15 June 1944. On that morning, the huge Allied armada was in place and after 0800, the first amphibious forces were sent on their way. Compared to the scope of previous Pacific operations, the scale of this one was huge, stretching over a four-mile area of beach and involving tens of thousands of men. Given the sheer size of the operation, there was much that might have gone wrong and there were good reasons for the nervousness of all

involved. At best, the Saipan operation would be over in a day or two; at worst, it might take weeks to conclude.

Although the initial landing of several thousand Marines was accomplished with few problems, it soon became clear that progress from the beaches to the interior was going to be slow. Despite the previous bombardment of coastal batteries and other installations, Japanese forces under the command of General Saito were sufficiently well dug in on high ground overlooking the loading areas to extract heavy casualties from the invaders and as if this was not problematic enough, American submarines reported the menacing presence of a large Japanese task force, seemingly headed for the area of the Marianas, on 16 June.

Spruance had good cause to be concerned about this enemy task force which had orders to engage and destroy the American fleet adjacent to Saipan. Although his own forces were superior in numbers to the enemy, Spruance had to maintain his support of the amphibious operation while preparing to do battle with the enemy and that more or less eliminated his numerical advantage and certainly limited his freedom of movement. Fortunately, he had adequate warning of the imminence of an enemy attack

Right: The Japanese carrier *Zuikaku,* accompanied by two destroyers, under heavy aerial attack at the Battle of the Philippine Sea. She was badly damaged during this action.

Above : A Japanese twin-engine bomber makes a spectacular crash into the sea over US escort carriers during the Battle of the Philippines Sea, known as the Great Marianas Turkey Shoot.
Right : The 16-inch guns of the battleship *Iowa* (BB. 61) bombard Tinian during June 1944.

so as to be able to deploy the forces under his command to maximum advantage.

The size of the Japanese task force; nine carriers, five battleships, thirteen cruisers and 28 destroyers, forced Spruance and Turner to postpone preliminary operations on Guam, which would have drained their strength, until after confrontation with Admiral Ozawa. This was probably just as well given the slow progress being made on Saipan thanks to the tenacity of the Japanese. As events were proved, the Allies could ill afford to dilute its manpower on the island.

It was clear from the size of the Japanese task force that they were prepared for a Waterloo in the Philippine Sea and postwar examination of Japanese materials confirms

this. Dozens of ships and hundreds of land-based aircraft were committed to what was hoped would be the last decisive naval battle of the Pacific War. The Japanese had been husbanding their resources for such a battle for many months and had not engaged American forces in any large-scale contest since Bougainville. While the American command did not know the precise nature of Ozawa's strategy, it was clearly understood that if Ozawa was roundly defeated the back of the Imperial Navy would be broken. The unforeseen intrusion of enemy naval forces provided the opportunity.

It had originally been the intention of the Japanese to engage the American fleet in the Palau Islands close to their bases but the Saipan landing dictated a change in plan. While the Japanese command lacked precise knowledge of the details of Operation Forager, once their intelligence spotted the massive build up of Allied forces it was not difficult for them to guess their enemy's target. Accordingly, Ozawa was dispatched posthaste to the Marianas to

engage and destroy the enemy, hopefully before he established a firm toehold on Saipan. What Ozawa did not know was that Spruance had a sufficient fix on the Japanese task force to allow for adequate protection of the landings, while also permitting him to deploy his carriers in a more than defensive posture.

On 17 June Spruance announced his battle plan to his lieutenants. It

A Grumman F6F-3 Hellcat lands on the *Lexington* (CV. 16 ex-*Cabot*), June 1944.

Above: The smoke rises as US carrier planes hit the Ushi Point airfield on Tinian June 1944.

called for Admirals Willis Lee and Marc Mitscher to concentrate their attention on enemy carrier forces and capital ships and pursue them vigorously. Details of such pursuit were to be left up to Lee and Mitscher as they saw fit. The only limitation imposed by Spruance was that Saipan

The wounded pilot of an F6F Hellcat is helped out of his aircraft on the *Essex* (CV. 9).

138

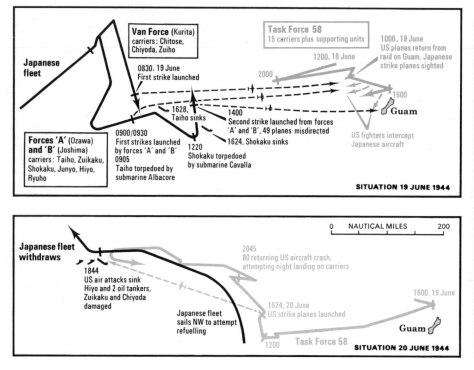

Map labels (Situation 19 June 1944):

Japanese fleet

Van Force (Kurita) carriers: Chitose, Chiyoda, Zuiho

Task Force 58 — 15 carriers plus supporting units

1200, 18 June

1000, 19 June US planes return from raid on Guam. Japanese strike planes sighted

2000

0830, 19 June First strike launched

1600

Guam

1628, Taiho sinks

1400 Second strike launched from forces 'A' and 'B', 49 planes misdirected

Forces 'A' (Ozawa) and 'B' (Joshima) carriers: Taiho, Zuikaku, Shokaku, Junyo, Hiyo, Ryuho

0900/0930 First strikes launched by forces 'A' and 'B' 0905 Taiho torpedoed by submarine Albacore

1220 Shokaku torpedoed by submarine Cavalla

1624, Shokaku sinks

US fighters intercept Japanese aircraft

SITUATION 19 JUNE 1944

Map labels (Situation 20 June 1944):

Japanese fleet withdraws

0 NAUTICAL MILES 200

1844 US air attacks sink Hiyo and 2 oil tankers, Zuikaku and Chiyoda damaged

2045 80 returning US aircraft crash, attempting night landing on carriers

Japanese fleet sails NW to attempt refuelling

1624, 20 June US strike planes launched

1600, 19 June

Guam

1200 Task Force 58

SITUATION 20 JUNE 1944

was to be protected at all cost even if it meant disengagement from the enemy. That caveat aside, Lee and Mitscher were given *carte blanche* to do what was necessary.

With Spruance's instruction in hand, Lee and Mitscher watched and waited for the enemy, hoping to find Ozawa before he found them. After searching in vain for the enemy on 18 June it was decided to stage a series of raids against Japanese air fields on Guam, in anticipation that Ozawa would be relying on land-based aircraft to support his attack. At about 0830 on 19 June the first mission was sent aloft. As this mission was returning from Guam, American intelligence detected the presence of large numbers of enemy aircraft heading toward Mitscher's carrier group. The Battle of the Philippine Sea had begun.

Thanks to the advance warning of the imminence of attack, Mitscher was able to clear the decks of his carriers

and provide an unanticipated 'welcome' for the enemy. When the first wave of Japanese aircraft reached the vicinity of the 5th Fleet at about 1030 they were greeted by an equal number of Americans who proceeded to decimate them. Two-thirds of the Japanese force were shot down and none of the surviving planes was able to reach their targets.

There was no time to gloat over the destruction of 45 enemy aircraft for even as this battle raged, a second wave of Japanese planes was headed toward the 5th Fleet and this attack group was twice the size of the first. Thanks again to the advance warning provided by radar, Mitscher's men were ready for this attack and were able to stop the enemy short of his mark, inflicting very heavy losses on him in the process. What is more, as US aircraft were pulverizing the Japanese, American submarines extracted an even greater toll from Ozawa, torpedoing and

sinking the carriers *Taiho* and *Shokaku*. It was a banner day for the United States Navy!

Ozawa launched two more raids from his three still operative carriers but these proved no more successful than the first two. Of 129 planes involved in these attacks, 74 were downed by American aircraft and more might have been destroyed had one of the raiding parties not proceeded to the wrong attack point. By the end of the day Ozawa had lost about 350 planes not to say anything of the toll of ground-based planes on Guam and elsewhere in the Marianas. When the sun set on 19 June, the Battle of the Philippine Sea was over, at least insofar as the Japanese were concerned.

Having sustained unusually heavy losses, Ozawa ordered a rapid retreat which commenced shortly after 2200. Mitscher made no concerted effort to pursue the fleeing enemy that night and it was not until the following morning that the 5th Fleet began to actively pursue the enemy. American reconnaissance craft caught up with the enemy on the evening of 20 June when a nighttime attack was staged. During this encounter the Japanese lost yet another carrier, the *Hiyo*, and over 60 planes. This was the final en-

Above left : Battle of the Phillipine Sea.
Above : Gun captain opens up the breech of his 16-inch gun.
Above right : Grumman TBF Avengers crowd the deck of the escort carrier *Santee* (CVE. 29), Guam, June 1944.

Left : Crew of the battleship *New Mexico* (BB. 40) line up for chow during a lull in the shore bombardment off Guam in July 1944.
Right : Some of the *New Mexico*'s 5-inch/.25 cal AA guns fire. She escaped Pearl Harbor, and her Class was the most modern of the older battleships.

Above left : Units of the Fast Carrier Group, TF 58.3 come under attack during the Battle of the Philippine Sea. It comprised the carriers *Enterprise* (CV. 6), *Lexington* (CV. 16), *Princeton* (CVL. 23) and *San Jacinto* (CVL. 30).
Above right : Gunners and radiomen relax before the strike on Guam in July 1944 on board the light carrier *Monterey* (CVL. 26).
Below : Before the next step from the Marianas to the Philippines the US had to take the Palau Islands. This Grumnan Avenger TBF torpedo bomber was the first US plane to land on Peleliu in September 1944.

counter of the Battle of the Philippine Sea. Spruance and Mitscher refused to venture further away from Saipan to pursue the enemy.

Despite Ozawa's defeat in the Battle of the Philippine Sea, the Japanese refused to surrender the Marianas. The Battle of Saipan continued for two weeks before the island was secured. In defending Saipan the Japanese had spent 25,000 lives and extracted 3500 deaths and casualties from the Marines. Once again, the enemy demonstrated his determined and suicidal willingness to resist, a fact that was to have an important bearing on American thinking and decision-making in 1945.

After a pause of several weeks American forces pushed on from Saipan to Tinian, landing there on 24 July. Compared to the ordeal they suffered on Saipan, the Tinian campaign was a 'picnic.' It took only a week to capture the island. At the same time, another amphibious group assaulted Guam. The campaign there lasted considerably longer than the one on Tinian but thanks to the reinforcement of the Guam invasion group by one division and the regular bombardment of Japanese positions which commenced three weeks before D-Day on 21 July, Guam was secured with casualties that were heavy but not as bad as they might have been, especially when one considers the size of the island and the strength of enemy forces on it.

Above: Gunners of the 805th Engineer Aviation Battalion fire machine guns from the deck of a Landing Ship Tank on their way to the Marianas.

On 12 August 1944 the American flag was once again raised over Guam and with that act Operation Forager had come to a close. The Marianas campaign had been a disaster for the Japanese from a military point of view but it also had significant political consequences, forcing the resignation of Hideki Tojo and his government. Although admission of defeat was still not an admissible option in Tokyo there was little doubt there that the tide had definitely turned. But the Japanese would fight on for yet another year before accepting the condition of unconditional surrender that had become the axiom of the Allies in 1943.

LSTs (Landing Ship, Tank) land cargo on one of the invasion beaches at low tide during the first days of the Normandy landings. On the beach is a convoy of halftracks preparing for action.

Neptune and Overlord

Operations Torch and Husky, however successful, had merely been diversionary at least insofar as many American military leaders were concerned. It had long been their contention that a serious effort to defeat Germany required a cross-Channel invasion of France after which Allied armies would slowly but surely carry the war back to Germany. Unfortunately for Generals Marshall and Eisenhower and others who held this view the British, whose participation in any such operation was absolutely vital, showed little or no enthusiasm for such a venture.

British opposition to the proposed assault on Fortress Europa was both emotional and pragmatic. Memories of the bloodletting of World War I were sufficiently fresh to dampen British willingness to consent to another continental confrontation, particularly against an enemy who seemed to spare no effort to protect his new found gains. In this regard, Churchill's response to American calls for a cross-Channel operation was more than emotional. He and his colleagues understood only too well that the Allies had neither the technical expertise nor the manpower and equipment to successfully execute a return to the continent in 1942 or 1943. Fortunately for the Allies, this view was presented with sufficient vigor by the British to prevail. As learned in Sicily and even more so in Italy proper, it would not be an easy matter to breach the Atlantic Wall.

The reservations of the British notwithstanding, American military leaders continued to press for a cross-Channel operation and at the Casablanca Conference in January 1943 they secured a promise that such an operation would take place the following year. Accordingly, an Allied Planning Staff was established in March 1943 and a British officer, General Frederick Morgan, was named to head this staff until such time as the Combined Chiefs named a Supreme Allied Commander at which time Morgan would become his Chief of Staff. Morgan and his staff of several

hundred established their headquarters in London.

By the end of May 1943 a D-Day of 1 May 1944 was set for the cross-Channel hop, but the places where Allied forces were to land remained undecided as did the matter of who was to command the expedition. There were two landing options available. Allied troops might be landed in the area of the Pas-de-Calais or along the Normandy coast between Caen and the Cotentin Peninsula. Although the Pas-de-Calais area was closer to England and contained better ports than one might find along the Normandy coast it was very heavily

defended. If the Germans expected the Allies to attempt a landing in France, it would be here. Consequently, despite the numerous problems inherent in conducting a large operation along the Normandy coast, Allied military leaders decided to take their risks with what was sometimes called the Calvados or Normandy operation. After June 1943, all planning for Operation Neptune/Overlord was based upon the notion of Normandy landings.

Having determined a tentative D-Day for Operation Overlord and decided upon the site for the Allied landings, it was necessary to select a

Above left : The old battleships *Nevada* (BB. 36) left, and *Texas* (BB. 45) before D-Day, June 1944.

Above : The forward 14-inch guns of the *Nevada* fire on shore positions at Utah Beach. The *Nevada* was torpedoed and beached at Pearl Harbor and was recommissioned in 1942 after repairs. She participated in the actions at Attu, Southern France, Iwo Jima and at Okinawa (where she was hit by a kamikaze on 26 March 1945) in addition to the Normandy landings.

Right : Navy Squadron VCS-7 exchanged its Curtiss SOC Seagulls for Spitfires for gunfire spotting during the Normandy landings.

Below : Minesweepers explode mines off Utah Beach on the morning of D-Day. The new 'oyster' or pressure mine proved a formidable obstacle.

Supreme Commander for their operation. It was clear from the outset that the Supreme Commander was to be an American officer; it was less clear which officer would be chosen for the assignment. Two men, George Marshall and Dwight Eisenhower, were prime candidates for the assignment. Marshall had seniority in rank and length of service but Eisenhower had more battle experience and had proved himself an able coordinator in Operations Torch and Husky. By all odds Marshall should have got the job, but in the end President Roosevelt succumbed to the lobbying of senior American military and naval leaders who felt Marshall could better serve the Allied cause by remaining in Washington and the appointment went to Eisenhower.

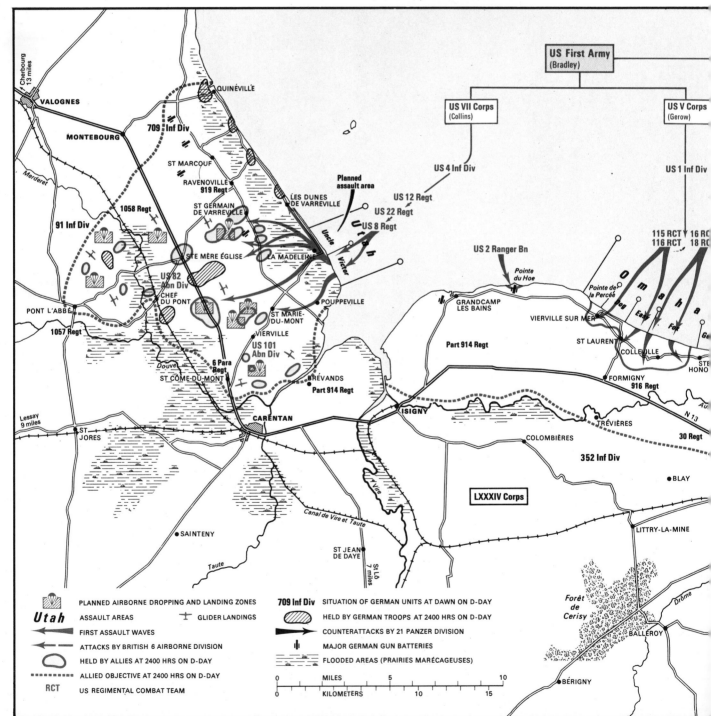

US First Army (Bradley)		

US VII Corps (Collins)	**US V Corps** (Gerow)

US 4 Inf Div

US 1 Inf Div

US 12 Regt

US 22 Regt

US 8 Regt

US 2 Ranger Bn

115 RCT   16 RC
116 RCT   18 RC

709 Inf Div

91 Inf Div

1058 Regt

1057 Regt

6 Para Regt

US 82 Abn Div

US 101 Abn Div

Part 914 Regt

Part 914 Regt

916 Regt

30 Regt

352 Inf Div

LXXXIV Corps

919 Regt

Legend

Utah — ASSAULT AREAS

— FIRST ASSAULT WAVES

— ATTACKS BY BRITISH 6 AIRBORNE DIVISION

— HELD BY ALLIES AT 2400 HRS ON D-DAY

----- ALLIED OBJECTIVE AT 2400 HRS ON D-DAY

RCT — US REGIMENTAL COMBAT TEAM

PLANNED AIRBORNE DROPPING AND LANDING ZONES

✝ GLIDER LANDINGS

709 Inf Div — SITUATION OF GERMAN UNITS AT DAWN ON D-DAY

HELD BY GERMAN TROOPS AT 2400 HRS ON D-DAY

COUNTERATTACKS BY 21 PANZER DIVISION

MAJOR GERMAN GUN BATTERIES

FLOODED AREAS (PRAIRIES MARÉCAGEUSES)

MILES 0 — 5 — 10

KILOMETERS 0 — 10 — 15

147

Eisenhower's appointment was announced at the Cairo Conference in December 1943 by which time his associates in this venture had also been chosen. Admiral Bertram Ramsay, RN, was to be Commander of the Naval Expeditionary Force; Air Marshal Sir Trafford Leigh-Mallory, RAF, would be Commander of Allied Air Forces and General Sir Bernard Montgomery was to be Eisenhower's deputy and chief lieutenant. These men and their subordinates were to be responsible for the largest and most dangerous

Far left: LCM (Landing Craft, Mechanized) comes alongside a transport, to evacuate casualties, 6 June 1944.
Left: Members of a Coast Guard-manned LST (Landing Ship, Tank) during the approach to Normandy on D-Day, 6 June.

amphibious operation in the history of warfare.

Although primary responsibility for driving the Germans out of France lay with the Army, the Allied navies had to bear the initial burden of transporting hundreds of thousands of men and their supplies and equipment across the Channel – no mean feat! There were many problems to deal with and obstacles to overcome in this regard, not the least of which were shortages of landing craft and the absence of good harbors, save for Cherbourg, which might take weeks to secure, on the French side. These problems were solved by Allied ingenuity and American economic resources. Artificial harbors or 'Mulberries' were developed by the British which could be towed across the

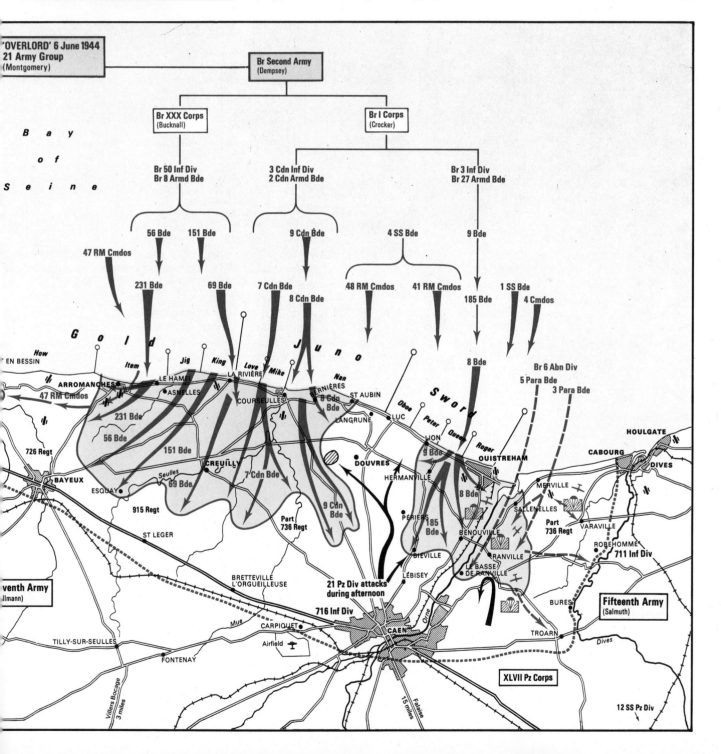

Channel and put in place off the Normandy coast to insure the uninterrupted flow of supplies and equipment. The United States for its part increased production quotas for landing craft of all kinds, to insure that the operation would not have to be canceled for lack of necessary weaponry and ships.

By February 1944 the Planning Staff had developed an outline for Operation Overlord which was slightly modified and adapted by Eisenhower and his associates. This plan called for a two-pronged Allied assault on the Normandy coast and if possible a smaller but simultaneous landing in southern France to open up a 'second front' to be known as Operation Anvil. American and British forces were to be landed at five beachheads stretching from just southeast of Cherbourg to the mouth of the Orne River. US

Forces would be responsible for Utah and Omaha beaches in the west; British forces would be responsible for three adjacent beachheads to the east, Gold, Juno and Sword. In sum, five divisions were to be carried to France during Operation Neptune, the first phase of Operation Overlord.

As Commander of the Western Naval Task Force, Rear Admiral Alan Kirk was the principal American naval officer involved in Operation Neptune. It was his mission to carry General Omar Bradley's First Army to France. With the exception of H Kent Hewitt, there was not a flag officer in the Atlantic Fleet more conversant with amphibious warfare. Furthermore, he had considerable experience in dealing with his British counterparts in the Royal Navy, a necessary 'diplomatic' prerequisite in such a complicated operation.

Top left : Troops in an LCVP (Landing Craft, Vehicles, Personnel) head for Omaha Beach on D-Day, 6 June 1944. LCVPs carried (as a rule) 36 troops and 1 vehicle or 5 tons of cargo.
Above : LCI-553 and LCI-410 (Landing Craft, Infantry) land troops on Omaha Beach.
Top right : Troops from USS LCI-412 land on Omaha Beach. Broached halftracks are pinned down on the shore.
Right : LSTs (Landing Ships, Tank) offer reinforcements and supplies to those already ashore at Omaha Beach.

Admiral Kirk set up his headquarters in London near the American Embassy but separate from Admiral Ramsay's offices. Despite the physical distance between the headquarters of the two men, they worked closely together and coordinated their efforts carefully. Working together on a project involving thousands of ships and even more men was an undertaking which might have failed but for the compatibility of the Allied naval commanders.

Below : The battleship *Arkansas* (BB. 33) supports the landings at Omaha Beach. The *Arkansas* had been in the Atlantic in 1941, and after D-Day went out to the Pacific for the landings on Iwo Jima and Okinawa.

The most serious question facing Kirk, Ramsay and Eisenhower was the matter of redefining D-Day and H-Hour for the operation. Although the date of the landings had originally been set for 1 May 1944, they had to be postponed several weeks in order to allow time for construction and delivery of additional landing craft. Meteorologists advised Allied commanders that two possible sets of dates were available the following month, 5–7 and 18–20 June and even then weather conditions and tides would be far from perfect. Because of the fear of enemy detection of American plans the earlier set of dates was chosen. This done, preliminary operations commenced.

Of the operations prior to Operation Neptune, none were more intensive than intelligence efforts to estimate enemy strength and deployment and subsequent aerial attacks on select enemy strongholds. While German defenses in Normandy were known to be less formidable than in the Pas-de-Calais they were significant, perhaps even more than the Allies were to

assume, particularly in the vicinity of Omaha Beach. Things might have been worse, however, had Hitler listened more seriously to the arguments of Rommel who predicted the possibility of an Allied operation in Normandy. In view of the relative weakness of the Luftwaffe and German Navy at this time such barriers as

Far left: Troops enjoy a brief respite on Omaha Beach shortly after the first landings, 6 June 1944. Note the number and variety of Landing Craft in the background.
Below: Army trucks move inland from Omaha Beach in early June 1944. A Rhino ferry is just offshore and ships are being positioned so that they can be scuttled and then used as a Gooseberry breakwater.

could be thrown up in front of the Atlantic Wall were the only defense the Germans had available.

Crucial to the success of Neptune/Overlord was an elaborate hoax involving General George Patton and a phantom invasion force 'stationed' along the east coast of England across from the Pas-de-Calais. Allied intelligence, being aware of the conviction of von Rundstedt and Hitler that the Pas-de-Calais area was likely to be the site of Allied landings, established this dummy force to confirm Nazi convictions and floated false reports through various agents to further reinforce this idea. So realistic were the mock bases of Patton's army that German aerial reconnaissance further confirmed the reports of German spies in England, almost all of whom were double agents.

The German command in France was almost entirely taken in by this deception. As a result, 19 German divisions remained stationed around the Pas-de-Calais despite appeals from Field Marshal Rommel that some of them be dispatched to Normandy.

Left : A convoy of LCIs en route to Normandy. The 20mm guns belong to the *Ancon* (ACG-4), the Amphibious Force Flagship. LCIs carried 200+ men to beachheads from offshore transports or from advance bases.
Right : A LCA wreathed in smoke at Omaha Beach.

One must wonder what might have happened if the Germans had not fallen victim to the Patton ploy and accepted the judgment of Rommel instead of von Rundstedt.

While a great effort had been made to deceive the Germans an even greater one was made to maintain absolute secrecy with regard to the build-up of Allied manpower and bases along the Channel coast from Falmouth to Newhaven. To this end extraordinary measures were taken, including evacuation of whole hamlets and close scrutiny and control of access into and out of the staging areas where well over one million American and British troops were waiting for their ride across the Channel. Given such a concentration of manpower and supplies, there was always the possibility of detection by the enemy. It is no wonder that Eisenhower and his staff were nervous about putting off Neptune/Overlord

Below left : The 1912 vintage battleship *Texas* (BB. 35) off Cherbourg, on 25 June 1944. Although unfit for front line duty her ten 14-inch guns could soften German defenses.
Below : A crippled Coast Guard-manned LCI-85 off Omaha Beach, 6 June 1944.

any longer than absolutely necessary.

By 1 June 1944 Allied preparations were almost complete. If the weather held, convoys would start forming on 3 June to be joined shortly thereafter by their escorts. While the ships were loaded with men and supplies, mine sweepers would clear paths through to the French coast. The Allied armada would leave England on 4 June in order to rendezvous in time for D-Day on 5 June.

As had happened so frequently in the planning of previous amphibious operations during the war the weather proved to be un-cooperative, forcing Allied leaders to consider delaying the entire operation. As 3 June dawned weather conditions became increasingly menacing. Worse still the short

range forecast for the next few days did not promise much relief. Eisenhower, Ramsay, Montgomery, Kirk *et al*, met several times on the third and fourth to consider what to do. After considerable soul-searching, it was decided to postpone D-Day to 6 June in the hope the bad weather might lift. If this delay of one day did not provide enough time, the entire operation would have to be postponed for at least two weeks. As one might imagine a tense situation prevailed at Southwick House, Ramsay's HQ and the nerve center of the operation.

Luck was to be with the Allies. A break in the weather which had been predicted by some staff meteorologists materialized on 5 June, permitting the operation to proceed. In the end it was

Above : LCTs land supplies on a Normandy invasion beachhead. In the background is a Gooseberry breakwater of surplus ships and a floating wave barrier.
Left : Long lines of men and material stream ashore in Northern France.

probably fortuitious that the weather had been so bleak because the enemy would never expect an attack in such adverse conditions. Indeed, this was precisely the feeling among German officers many of whom, including Rommel, had left the front for brief holidays or to attend to other matters during the first week in June, secure in the knowledge that bad weather precluded a cross-Channel attack.

General Eisenhower ordered Operation Neptune to proceed at 0415 on 5 June. Within minutes after this decision was relayed to the naval task forces the first convoys moved out. Ramsay's plan for the passage across the Channel called for the two principal task forces to converge near the Isle of Wight at a rendezvous affectionately called Piccadilly Circus, a large circle some five miles in radius. From

Below : US troops land on the beaches of Normandy shortly after the Allied Invasion, 6 June 1944.

Piccadilly Circus the five groups which comprised the two task forces would proceed towards the French coast where the five cleared lanes would further subdivide into ten; two per group. If all went according to plan the Allied armada would reach the enemy shore before dawn on the morning of 6 June, separating and proceeding to the five landing areas designated Utah, Omaha, Gold, Juno and Sword.

Considering the complexity of the operation and the congestion of ships of all kinds and sizes, the first crossings went remarkably well; so well in fact that the enemy did not detect the presence of a large Allied Force before 0300 by which time most of the transports were in place off the French coast. Although Admiral Krancke, the senior German naval commander, sounded an alert and ordered German forces to repel an invasion shortly after 0300, no action was taken until after 0500 when German batteries opened fire on Allied ships. This two-hour delay permitted the successful completion of phase one of Operation Neptune.

To insure that the enemy could not

Above: The shattered hull of the minesweeper *Tide* (AM. 125) sinks off Omaha Beach after hitting a mine, 7 June 1944. Patrol Torpedo Boat *PT-509* and the minesweeper *Pheasant* (AM. 61) stand by.
Below: LCVPs (Landing Craft, Vehicles, Personnel) cruise off the coast of Normandy 10 June 1944, with transports in the background.

easily rush reinforcements to the beachheads, over 10,000 paratroops were dropped behind the enemy's coastal defenses several hours before H-Hour. Although this effort was not a total success thanks to the obstacles which the Germans had installed and their early detection of the drops, the Allies once again had fortune on their side. The German command, seemingly convinced that these drops were a diversionary effort only, refused to move forces away from the Pas-de-

Calais and even after it had become clear that a major assault was underway, the Germans seemed preoccupied with the paratroops, particularly in the Utah Beach area, much to the good fortune of the Americans.

Shortly before sunrise, German batteries opened fire on Allied ships forcing Ramsay and Kirk to begin bombardment of enemy installations somewhat earlier than had been planned. A powerful combination of naval artillery and support aircraft had been provided with the most current information the Allies had relative to coastal defenses in the landing areas, and were able to silence many of the shore batteries and disrupt others before the first landings were made. They were not, however, able to destroy installations about which they had no information. Unfortunately, there were many of these, particularly in the Omaha sector. The Americans at Utah Beach fared considerably better.

At 0630, the first wave of landing craft hit the beaches at Utah. The run in from the transports was long and unpleasant given the din and smoke from exploding bombs and shells on the shore. Fortunately, the first troops to land encountered little or no enemy resistance due perhaps to the fact that they had landed several thousand yards away from the designated landing area. Capitalizing on this 'error,' other landing craft were diverted to the new beachhead, thus avoiding German machine gun emplacements at the original site.

In many respects Utah Beach proved to be the easiest of the five target areas to secure. In addition to the lack of initial resistance to the landing there were few mines or other booby traps and, given the brief absence of enemy machine gun fire and shelling, American demolition experts were able to defuse these. As a result, the first assault on Utah Beach went off with almost textbook precision. By the

time the second wave of Americans reached the shore and German resistance commenced, supply depots were operative inland and all was in order on the beaches. Over 20,000 men and nearly 2000 vehicles had been landed with few losses.

If the landings at Utah Beach were executed without incident, the Omaha landings were fraught with obstacles and problems. Omaha Beach contained just about every booby trap and defense preparation that German military

Men of the US Navy dismantle a German remote-controlled miniature tank on Utah Beach on the 11 June 1944. An open amphtrac (Landing Vehicle, Tracked) awaits in the background.

technology could conceive from concertina wire, mines and pikes to giant hedgehogs of steel bars. Furthermore, at least two regiments of German forces were positioned behind these defenses to welcome the Americans.

In retrospect it is evident that Allied intelligence had clearly underestimated

the enemy's strength at Omaha. One consequence of this was that there was insufficient time allocated for preliminary naval and aerial bombardment which commenced only minutes before H-Hour. Very little damage was done to German positions in this brief attack. Thus, when the first American soldiers reached the shore just after 0630, they immediately encountered enemy fire and suffered heavy casualties.

Many men were lost to enemy machine guns and mines on the beach. An almost equal number were injured or drowned trying to wade ashore in several feet of water through obstacles of all kinds and also under heavy fire. Given the ferocity of German resistance, chaos and disorder reigned supreme at Omaha Beach for several hours. It was not until late afternoon that naval artillery and aerial strikes were able to silence the enemy sufficiently to permit the unloading of equipment and supplies and the regrouping of Army units. By this time 2000 men had been killed or wounded.

Despite the heavy toll in life and limb during the first hours of the landing at Omaha Beach, 32,000 troops reached the beach safely by the end of the day and many more were to follow in succeeding days. The Atlantic Wall had been breached but one cannot imagine what might have happened if the Germans had been expecting an American attack at Utah and Omaha.

The costly but successful landings at Utah and Omaha marked the end of the first phase of the cross-Channel operation and the beginning of phase two, a massive effort to consolidate and support the gains made by the Americans and their British counterparts at Gold, Juno and Sword. For the next several weeks the Navy and Royal Navy would be responsible for ferrying over larger amounts of supplies and heavy equipment, not to say anything of supplying necessary artillery support, all of this in the face of a last desperate effort of the German command to stave off the collapse of the Atlantic Wall.

At this time the Allies enjoyed absolute superiority over the enemy on the seas and in the air, making it impossible for Rommel and von Rundstedt to push them back to the sea in spite of several attempts to do so. First at Cherbourg and again at dozens of less important strongpoints, the Nazis made matters miserable for Allied troops, slowing the timetable of their advance, and extracting heavy casualties. In the end, however, the Allies prevailed, thanks in no small measure to the efforts of the Navy and the efficiency with which it carried out its allocated tasks in this, the largest amphibious operation in the history of warfare. Many difficult months of fighting still lay ahead but the die had been cast. From 6 June 1944 until V-E Day, the enemy was on the defensive. The beginning of the end had commenced.

Above: Navy beach battalion takes over a German trench on the Normandy beach, 11 June 1944.
Right: A Sherman tank with special air intakes for wading ashore lies in a shell-crater on a Normandy beach on 12 June 1944.
Below left: A US Navy Beachmaster unit directs incoming craft in the post-invasion build-up.
Below: A US Navy Communication Command on a Normandy beach, 11 June.
Bottom: Phoenix caissons for a Mulberry Harbor are towed into position, 14 June.

The enormous invasion fleet gathers before the
landings at Leyte.

Return to the Philippines

For years Douglas MacArthur had vowed to avenge America's defeat in the Philippines and return the Islands to American sovereignty. With the victory in the Battle of the Philippine Sea it was possible to translate this promise into a reality, but there were those who did not share MacArthur's sense of poetic justice and proposed alternatives to an attack on the Philippines. These men, including Admiral King and many of his subordinates in the Navy, suggested by-passing the Philippines entirely in favor of an attack on Formosa and the Ryukyu Islands from which the Allies would mount their final attack on Japan.

MacArthur, as might be expected, reacted with horror to the suggestion that the Philippines should be by-passed on the road back to Tokyo. This would not only be a breach of faith and trust, it made no sense from a strategic and tactical point of view. As MacArthur convincingly pointed out in July 1944 at a meeting with President Roosevelt and Admiral Nimitz, Formosa was so heavily protected that any attempt to secure that large island would make Guadalcanal and Tarawa look like picnics, costing the Allies more men and supplies than they were prepared to commit in the light of events in Europe and Eisenhower's needs there.

Thanks to the cogency of his argument and the force with which it was presented, MacArthur won a commitment from the President and Nimitz to a Philippine campaign. Two months later, at the Quebec Conference, details of this venture and a timetable for it were approved. As envisaged by the Combined Chiefs, the Philippines were to be liberated in several steps. First, Leyte was to be secured. Following this, Luzon might be invaded. If all went according to plan, Leyte was to be taken in October 1944 with Luzon to follow in November or December. As insurance for the success of the Leyte landings, Morotai and Peleliu were to be seized and used as advance bases.

Overall command of the Philippine campaign was divided between MacArthur and Nimitz. Neither Roosevelt nor the Joint Chiefs wished to become further embroiled in the rivalry between these two men by selecting one above the other for overall responsibility for this enormous undertaking. Such diplomacy may have had certain political advantages but it posed a number of logistical problems which might have been disastrous were it not for the willingness of those involved to subordinate their egos to a greater cause.

In preparing for the invasion of Leyte, Admiral Nimitz amassed an armada of over 1000 ships which were divided into the 3rd and 7th Fleets under the commands of Admirals Halsey and Kinkaid respectively. Included in these task forces were more than a dozen aircraft carriers and dozens of battleships and cruisers.

Above: Japanese carriers *Zuikaku* (center) and *Chitose* (background) and a destroyer in action during the Battle off Cape Engaño, 25 October 1944.
Right: A LCIR (Landing Craft, Infantry, Rocket) support ship fires her 5-inch rockets during the Leyte landings, 20 October 1944.
Far right: General MacArthur and President Osmena of the Philippines.

Below: The battleship *Colorado* (BB. 45) as she appeared in early October preparing for the invasion of Leyte Gulf. It should be noted that a wartime censor has obliterated her radar installations in this photograph.

Above : Coast Guard-manned LSTs (Landing Ships, Tank) unload at Leyte.
Left : PT-boats evade bombs from Japanese land-based aircraft defending Leyte Gulf.
Far right : The Allied Navies prepare to land at Leyte, 20 October 1944, an event which triggered the greatest naval battle in history.
Below : The destroyer *Heermann* lays smoke off Samar during the battle of Leyte.

Never before had such a large attack group been assembled in the Pacific and never before had the enemy been so ill-prepared to meet the Allied thrust.

The Battle of the Philippine Sea had almost broken the back of the Imperial Navy but the Japanese still had sufficient numbers of troops in the Philippines and air power in these islands and Formosa to pose real problems. That being the case, American aircraft spent the week from 10–17 October attacking Japanese installations on Taiwan and the Philippines. These raids took a very heavy toll of enemy aircraft. At least 600 Japanese aircraft were destroyed. In the battle that was to follow, the Americans enjoyed absolute air superiority both on land and on the seas.

On 17 October minesweepers began to clear channels into Leyte while Rangers were landed on several islands adjacent to Leyte Gulf. The following day, battleships and cruisers of the Support Group of the 7th Fleet launched an artillery barrage against enemy emplacements near the landing areas. By A-Day, 20 October, all was ready.

The first Americans waded ashore onto Leyte on 20 October, encountering little resistance and few obstacles or booby traps. In three days over 125,000 men and 225,000 tons of supplies were landed without incident. Although the amphibious assault had been carried out with textbook precision, no one in the American command imagined for a moment that this uncontested situation would last forever and they were right.

Defense of the Philippines was vital for the Japanese. If MacArthur was successful on Leyte and Luzon, Japanese forces in the islands would be trapped and the Imperial Navy

would be cut off from sources of petroleum in the Indies and elsewhere. Some response to the Allied Offensive was clearly in order but given their shortages of equipment and trained personnel, particularly pilots, Japanese military leaders had few options available.

In the light of their limited resources, only a surprise attack was likely to net the kind of results the Japanese hoped for, namely isolating American forces on Leyte and avenging their defeat in the Battle of the Philippine Sea. The Allied armada associated with the landings on Leyte was too large to attack frontally but if it could be caught off-guard as it disgorged its forces, a victory might be achieved. This was the Imperial Navy's only chance to turn the tide. Accordingly Admiral Ozawa and his staff prepared to surprise the enemy in Leyte Gulf.

The plan adopted by the Japanese called for a task force under the command of Vice-Admiral Kurita (Center Force) to sail through the San Bernardino Straits into Leyte Gulf and attack American transports while a second task force (Southern Group) under the joint command of Admirals Nishimura and Shima entered Leyte Gulf from the south through the Surigao Strait. A third task force of nearly plane-less aircraft carriers (Northern Group) under the command of Vice-Admiral Ozawa was to serve as a decoy to lure Halsey's 3rd Fleet up north and out of the way of the main action in Leyte Gulf.

Unfortunately for the Japanese, American submarines spotted Kurita's Center Force before it had penetrated Leyte Gulf and sank three ships before

relaying word of Kurita's whereabouts to the American command. Armed with this intelligence American carrier-based planes attacked Center Group the following day, 24 October, sinking one battleship and damaging several others, forcing Kurita to withdraw from the area.

Shima and Nishimura fared little better than Kurita. As luck would have it, their Southern Task Force was spotted moving toward the Surigao Strait. Responding to this intelligence, Admiral Kinkaid moved elements of the 7th Fleet into a position in front of the Strait where it emptied

Right : The heavy cruiser *Portland* (CA. 33) fires her forward 8-inch guns during the Leyte landings in October 1944.
Far right top : Army troops eat aboard the fast transport *Ward* (APD. 16). The *Ward* was a destroyer until January 1943 when she was converted to an amphibious transport, with troop accommodation in place of some boilers and armament.
Far right center : The *Downes* (DD. 375) bombards Marcus Island, 9 October 1944, in an attempt to create a diversion from Leyte.
Below : LSTs (Landing Ships, Tank) formed the backbone of the invasion fleet. Over 1000 were built and they carried small craft topside and tanks, vehicles, guns and cargo in a tunnel-like hold.

into Leyte Gulf. In an engagement reminiscent of the Battle of Tsushima Straits in 1905 with the sides reversed, the Japanese tried to plow through Surigao with disastrous consequences. Many enemy ships were destroyed including the battleships *Fuso* and *Yamashiro* after being caught between American battlelines forcing the abortion of the mission and the quick retreat of what remained of the Southern Task Force.

The United States Navy had thwarted the enemy's efforts to disrupt operations in Leyte Gulf but reports of a total rout of Japanese forces were exaggerated and led to serious consequences. Having disposed of the Japanese, or so it was thought, Halsey was sent north to take on Ozawa's 'dummy fleet,' leaving the San Bernardino Straits unprotected. Sailing through this vacuum undetected, Kurita's Center Group, supposedly destroyed on 24 October, entered Leyte Gulf and launched an attack on the unprotected escort carriers of the 7th Fleet.

Kurita's task force was formidable, including the super battleship *Yamato* with her 18-inch guns, the battleship *Nagato*, and the cruisers *Haguro, Chokai, Kumano, Chikuma, Tone* and *Suzuya*. Under ordinary circumstances, it would have been impossible for a force of escort carriers to survive a confrontation with such a force of capital ships. Fortunately for the Americans, however, Kurita had no air power to use against them, permitting Admiral Sprague to use the aircraft on his carriers as flying artillery pieces against superior Japanese forces without engaging enemy aircraft. Notwithstanding this fact, the odds still remained stacked in favor of the Japanese.

Although an SOS was sent out to the other American task forces to the south, the Battle of Samar was fought by Sprague's group alone, assisted only by such aircraft from other groups that were able to rush to Sprague's aid. The battleships and cruisers of Admirals Oldendorf and Lee were too far from the area to play a role in the fray. In the end the battle pitted air power against fire power.

Thanks to some confusion among Kurita and his commanders resulting from poor intelligence, Sprague was able to maneuver his ships out of close range of enemy guns so that air strikes could be safely launched. These carrier-based aircraft assisted by land-based planes flying from Tacloban Field on Leyte wreaked havoc on the enemy, sinking several cruisers and damaging the battleship *Nagato*. Fearing the loss of his entire task force, Kurita ordered a retreat shortly after noon on 25 October. The Japanese had once again been foiled but in the process, the USN also suffered heavy casualties losing two escort carriers and several destroyers.

While Sprague was contending with Kurita, Halsey finished off Ozawa's decoy force of four carriers, two converted carriers and their complements of about 100 planes. Given the absolute

Below: Captain T G W Settle (bareheaded) on the bridge of the heavy cruiser *Portland* (CA. 33) gives the order to open fire on Leyte, 20 October 1944.
Bottom: A gunner's mate cleans the after 5-inch guns of the destroyer *Brown* (DD. 546) following a night air action off Formosa, an assault which was concurrent with the actions off Leyte.

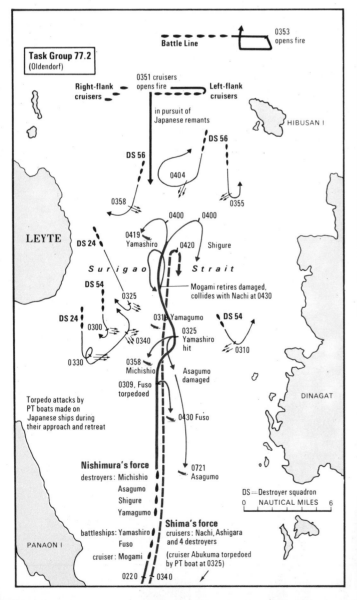

Task Group 77.2 (Oldendorf)

0353 Battle Line opens fire

Right-flank cruisers   0351 cruisers opens fire   **Left-flank cruisers**

HIBUSAN I

in pursuit of Japanese remnants

DS 56   DS 56
0404
0358   0355
0400   0400

LEYTE

0419 Yamashiro   0420 Shigure
DS 24

Surigao Strait

DS 54   Mogami retires damaged, collides with Nachi at 0430
0325
0318 Yamagumo   **DS 54**
DS 24   0325 Yamashiro hit   0310
0300
0340   Asagumo damaged
0330   DINAGAT
0358 Michishio
0309, Fuso torpedoed

Torpedo attacks by PT boats made on Japanese ships during their approach and retreat   0430 Fuso

0721 Asagumo

DS = Destroyer squadron
0   NAUTICAL MILES   6

Nishimura's force
destroyers: Michishio
Asagumo
Shigure
Yamagumo

Shima's force
cruisers: Nachi, Ashigara and 4 destroyers

battleships: Yamashiro
Fuso   (cruiser Abukuma torpedoed by PT boat at 0325)
cruiser: Mogami

PANAON I   0220   0340

air superiority of the 3rd Fleet, there was little that could be done by Ozawa to ward off disaster except to use anti-aircraft fire. In three successive strikes, American pilots destroyed four of Ozawa's six carriers while damaging another before the Battle of Cape Engano was broken off in the afternoon of 25 October.

The failure of the Imperial Navy's attack on the Allies at Leyte left the defense of the Philippine Islands to the Imperial Army and Air Force. Having lost the bulk of their fleet in the engagements with 3rd and 7th Fleets between 23–25 October, the Imperial Navy was no longer in a position to

challenge the USN. Without adequate naval forces, the Japanese had to resort to *kamikaze* or suicide attacks to neutralize the American Fleet.

The kamikazes made their debut in the Battle for Leyte; operating from land-based fields kamikaze pilots conducted suicide missions against American vessels, particularly aircraft carriers, from November 1944–January 1945. Locked into their bomb-filled planes, the kamikazes operated as human guided missiles crashing their planes into enemy ships. Thousands of young Japanese eventually volunteered for such suicide missions. They formed an elite corps which

The Japanese cruiser *Kumano* is bombed by planes of Task Force 38, 26 October 1944.

captivated Japanese public opinion but struck fear in the Allied heart.

Although it was difficult to defend against kamikaze attacks as Admiral Halsey was to find out, they did not prove to be a decisive factor in the Battle for Leyte. Of the dozens of ships involved in support of American forces on the island, less than a dozen vessels were damaged or destroyed by such attacks. It was not until the Lingayen

The destroyer *Hull* (DD. 350) leaves Puget Sound Navy Yard to join the fleet in the Pacific.

Above : LSMs (Landing Ship, Medium) approach the beach at Leyte, 20 October. These landing ships were faster and more maneuverable than LSTs.

landings in January 1945 that the kamikazes were to seriously threaten the American offensive in the Philippines.

Of more concern to MacArthur and Nimitz were Japanese efforts to reinforce their garrison on Leyte. Despite American control of Leyte Gulf by day, nightly Tokyo expresses reminiscent of Guadalcanal were successful in bringing reinforcements to the island, eventually raising the number of Japanese there to over 45,000 men. Although American forces in the area outnumbered the Japanese by almost three to one, the Japanese were dug in to stay. It took Lieutenant General Krueger's Sixth Army almost two months before Leyte could be safely in American hands, thus delaying the invasion of Luzon until after the new year.

There had never been any doubt in General MacArthur's mind that an invasion of Luzon should follow the Leyte campaign but, as pointed out earlier, Admiral King and others in the Navy did not share the General's enthusiasm for the liberation of the Philippines and continued to push for an alternative thrust into Formosa even after President Roosevelt had given the green light to the Leyte venture. It was not until the eve of the Leyte landings that the Joint Chiefs finally sanctioned landings on Luzon. This decision was made somewhat reluctantly after General Marshall confirmed MacArthur's estimate that the number of divisions which would be needed to secure Taiwan was beyond what the Army could spare for the Pacific Theater. The Luzon operation, on the other hand, would require no more men than had already been committed to taking Leyte.

Lingayen Bay was chosen to be the site for the landings on Luzon and 20 December 1944 was to be D-Day

for the assault. Given the slow progress of Sixth Army forces on Leyte, however, the timetable for the Lingayen Gulf landings had to be readjusted with the first landings re-scheduled for 9 January 1945 by which time it was hoped that Krueger's five divisions could be spared for the new operation. While the Sixth Army cleaned up in Leyte the Army Air Force, assisted by the Navy, ferried 28,000 men to Mindoro which was secured to provide air bases from which the AAF could support the Lingayen landings. With Mindoro in Allied hands, all was ready for the liberation of Luzon and Manila.

If the initial amphibious assault on Leyte had been carried out with little enemy resistance, the landings at Lingayen were a nightmare by comparison thanks to the reception provided by General Yamashita's forces on Luzon and the acceleration of kamikaze attacks on the landing forces. Between 1–9 January, kamikaze pilots constantly harassed the American fleet, successfully crashing many ships of

Right : The *Boston* (CA. 69), a *Baltimore* Class heavy cruiser. These 13,000-tonners were the most powerful cruisers in the world.

Admiral Oldendorf's advanced Support Group.

Although three out of every four kamikaze planes were shot down, it was impossible to completely thwart these suicide missions. Since kamikaze pilots often flew at very low altitudes, it was difficult to pick them up on radar thus providing early warning of their menacing presence. If the kamikaze were to be stopped, it would have to be done on the ground at the Luzon bases. Accordingly, massive airstrikes on Japanese bases on Luzon were

Right : The Japanese carrier *Zuiho* is attacked by planes from the *Enterprise* during the Battle off Cape Engaño, 25 October 1944. Note the deck camouflage suggesting a battleship's guns.
Center bottom : Japanese shells burst around Rear-Admiral Sprague's escort carriers.
Below : The *Darter* (SS. 227) after she had run aground off southwest Palawan during the Battle of Leyte Gulf.

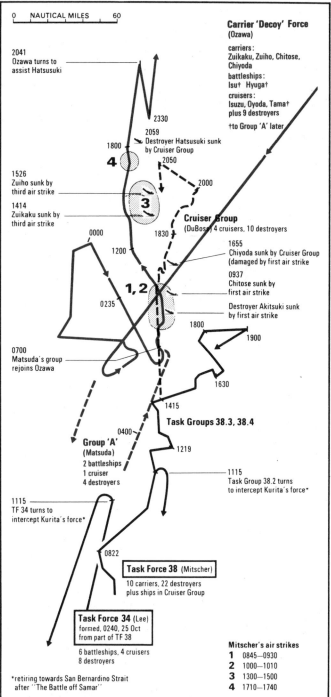

0 NAUTICAL MILES 60

Carrier 'Decoy' Force
(Ozawa)

carriers:
Zuikaku, Zuiho, Chitose,
Chiyoda
battleships:
Ise† Hyuga†
cruisers:
Isuzu, Oyoda, Tama†
plus 9 destroyers

†to Group 'A' later

2041
Ozawa turns to
assist Hatsusuki

2330

2059
Destroyer Hatsusuki sunk
by Cruiser Group

1800

2050

4

2000

1526
Zuiho sunk by
third air strike

3

1414
Zuikaku sunk by
third air strike

Cruiser Group
(DuBose) 4 cruisers, 10 destroyers

1655
Chiyoda sunk by Cruiser Group
(damaged by first air strike)

0000

1200

1830

0937
Chitose sunk by
first air strike

1, 2

0235

Destroyer Akitsuki sunk
by first air strike

1800

1900

0700
Matsuda's group
rejoins Ozawa

1630

1415

Task Groups 38.3, 38.4

0400

Group 'A'
(Matsuda)
2 battleships
1 cruiser
4 destroyers

1219

1115
Task Group 38.2 turns
to intercept Kurita's force*

1115
TF 34 turns to
intercept Kurita's force*

0822

Task Force 38 (Mitscher)

10 carriers, 22 destroyers
plus ships in Cruiser Group

Task Force 34 (Lee)
formed, 0240, 25 Oct
from part of TF 38

6 battleships, 4 cruisers
8 destroyers

*retiring towards San Bernardino Strait
after ''The Battle off Samar''

Mitscher's air strikes
1 0845—0930
2 1000—1010
3 1300—1500
4 1710—1740

Above : The Japanese battleship *Yamato* is hit by a bomb on the forecastle during the Battle of the Sibuyan Sea, 24 October 1944.
Far left : The battleship *Musashi* and other ships of Admiral Kurita's force come under air attack during the Battle of the Sibuyan Sea.
Left : Crew members of the sinking Japanese aircraft carrier *Zuikaku* cheer after the lowering of the imperial ensign during the Battle off Cape Engaño, 25 October 1944.
Below : A Grumman F6F Hellcat pulls out of a dive after chasing a 'Zeke' Mitsubishi A6M Zero which crashed into the small carrier *Suwannee* (CVE. 27) 25 October 1944 operating with the 7th Fleet.

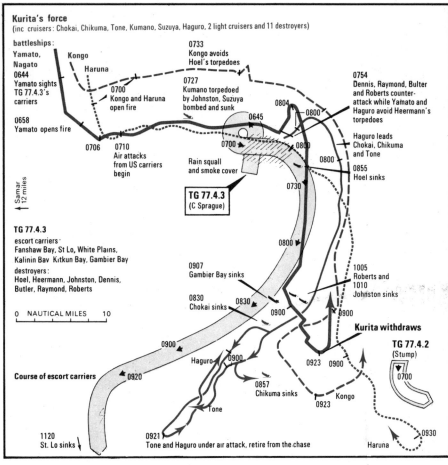

Kurita's force
(inc cruisers: Chokai, Chikuma, Tone, Kumano, Suzuya, Haguro, 2 light cruisers and 11 destroyers)

battleships:
Yamato,
Nagato
0644
Yamato sights
TG 77.4.3's
carriers
0658
Yamato opens fire

Kongo
Haruna

0733
Kongo avoids
Hoel's torpedoes

0700
Kongo and Haruna
open fire

0727
Kumano torpedoed
by Johnston, Suzuya
bombed and sunk

0754
Dennis, Raymond, Butler
and Roberts counter-
attack while Yamato and
Haguro avoid Heermann's
torpedoes

0645
0700
0710
Air attacks
from US carriers
begin

Rain squall
and smoke cover

0706

Samar
12 miles

TG 77.4.3
(C Sprague)

0804
0800
0800
0800
0730

Haguro leads
Chokai, Chikuma
and Tone

0855
Hoel sinks

TG 77.4.3
escort carriers:
Fanshaw Bay, St Lo, White Plains,
Kalinin Bay, Kitkun Bay, Gambier Bay
destroyers:
Hoel, Heermann, Johnston, Dennis,
Butler, Raymond, Roberts

0 NAUTICAL MILES 10

0907
Gambier Bay sinks

0830
Chokai sinks

0830

0800

0900

1005
Roberts and
1010
Johnston sinks

0900

Kurita withdraws

TG 77.4.2
(Stump)

Course of escort carriers

0920

Haguro

0900

0857
Chikuma sinks

Tone

0923

0900

Kongo

0923

0700

0930

Haruna

1120
St. Lo sinks

0921
Tone and Haguro under air attack, retire from the chase

Above left: The destroyer *Haraden* (DD. 585) after she was hit by a Japanese kamikaze while *en route* to Mindoro Island, 15 December 1944.

commenced after 9 January. By 14 January Japanese bases on Luzon were nearly all out of commission and Allied forces on the island were able to continue their progress without further kamikaze harassment.

From beginning to end, the liberation of Luzon was an ordeal. Although massive attacks had neutralized enemy air power, ground forces met with particularly stiff resistance from their Japanese counterparts. Although the Japanese command in the Philippines had no illusions about stopping the American advance in the Islands, they were determined to make the liberation of Luzon a costly one. General Yamashita husbanded all of the resources at his disposal for a long fight, retreating to the mountains while leaving some of his forces around Clark Field and Manila.

With Lingayen beach secured, Manila became the next target for American forces. Thousands of Ameri-

Left: The *Ward* (APD. 16), an old destroyer converted to a transport, was hit and sunk by a kamikaze in Ormoc Bay on 15 December, 1944. She had fired the first shot of the Pacific War at Pearl Harbor.
Far left center: A Japanese Yokosuka D4Y 'Judy' makes a kamikaze dive on the *Essex* (CV. 9) off the Philippines.
Far left bottom: Two Japanese *Ise* Class battleships took part in the Battle of Cape Engaño.

can nationals were still prisoners in or near the city. Lacking proper rations of food and water, they might die if liberation was postponed but even if this were not the case, there were often other reasons why MacArthur was so keen to re-occupy the city, not the least of which was the General's sense of poetic justice. His arguments about the urgency of liberating Manila were presented so forcefully that no one dared take exception to them, particularly in light of the fact that the Japanese were not expected to make the city their 'last stand.' Unfortunately, this was not to be the case.

Although General Yamashita had decided to evacuate Manila and abandon the city to the Americans, Admiral Iwabuchi, who commanded in excess of 20,000 sailors in the Manila area, refused to obey his superior's orders and was responsible for a prolonged battle for control of Manila which resulted in heavy casualties and the virtual destruction of much of the city. When American forces finally took the city in February, much of Old Manila lay in ruins.

Manila was occupied by American forces in February but it was not until the end of July that General MacArthur was able to announce the return of American rule to the rest of the Islands. By that time, the major confrontation between the Allies and Japan had moved to Iwo Jima and the Ryukyu Islands. There was little time to savor the return to the Philippines.

Japan Subdued

These Japanese Prisoners of War on Guam, have just heard that the Emperor Hirohito announced Japan's unconditional surrender, 15 August 1945.

178

At the time when the Joint Chiefs gave their blessings to the invasion of the Philippines, they also ordered Admiral Nimitz to prepare for operations in the Bonin and Ryukyu Islands following the successful occupation of Luzon. Iwo Jima and Okinawa, the targets of this offensive, were considered vital way stations from which the final assault on Japan would be launched.

Originally scheduled for 20 January and 1 March 1945 respectively, the Bonin and Ryukyu campaigns had to be postponed several times as Allied forces remained bogged down in the Philippines thanks to the fierce resistance of Japanese garrisons on Leyte and Luzon. Despite such unanticipated delays, preparation for landings on Iwo Jima and Okinawa continued with D-Days rescheduled for mid-February and early April.

Iwo Jima was less heavily defended than Okinawa or so Allied planners thought; hence, it was selected to be their first target. Once secured, Iwo Jima would provide emergency landing facilities for B-29s, flying to and from Japan. Iwo Jima would also provide bases for fighter escorts accompanying the B-29s on their missions. Such planes lacked the range to make the round trip from the Marianas to Japan and back without refueling.

In anticipation of a 19 February landing on Iwo Jima, American aircraft launched daily attacks on Japanese installations on that small island. These missions were flown from 1 January to the morning of the assault. As historians of the Pacific later frequently point out, Iwo Jima witnessed the heaviest bombardment of the Pacific War to that date. What they often fail to point out, however, is how ineffective such bombardment actually was.

Given the nature of their defenses on Iwo Jima, the Japanese were barely affected by the air raids launched against them. On Iwo Jima they had prepared an elaborate labyrinth of interconnecting caves and subterranean defenses which were almost impervious to aerial bombardment. The American command had little knowledge of the extent to which Iwo Jima had been turned into an impregnable fortress nor was it anticipated that the Japanese would defend the island to the last man. Nimitz and those immediately responsible for the amphibious operation, namely Turner, Mitscher and Spruance, did not expect the seizure of Iwo Jima to be easy but none of them would have predicted that this operation would be among the most brutal of the war.

In planning for the invasion of Iwo Jima, 5th Fleet commanders had the luxury for the first time in the Pacific

Above: Japanese carrier *Amagi* which was sunk in harbor on 24 July 1945.
Above right: The *Nevada* bombards Iwo Jima on 19 February 1945. The battleship *North Carolina* (BB. 55) is in the background.
Above far right: Mount Suribachi under fire from US ships on D-Day, Iwo Jima.
Center right: During the landings on Iwo Jima the US landing craft were subjected to intensive fire. Injured and dead guncrews lie on the deck as another ship pulls alongside to give aid.
Center far right: The forward end of the flightdeck of the old carrier *Saratoga* (CV. 3) burns after receiving a direct hit from a kamikaze.
Below: LSIs of the invasion force approach Iwo Jima.

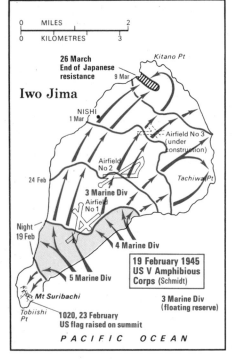

War of mapping out a major amphibious assault without fear of Japanese naval intervention. The Imperial Navy or what remained of it had been virtually destroyed near Leyte Gulf in October 1944. All that remained of this once great navy were a few submarines and a handful of capital ships now stationed in 'safe' ports in Japan. Only the kamikazes might pose some hazard to the mission and this was taken care of by a series of pre-landing attacks on bases from which such suicide squadrons could be launched. Never before had conditions seemed more propitious for a landing on enemy held territory.

As D-Day approached, 5th Fleet Bombardment Group joined in the pre-landing preliminaries while the rest of the attack force steamed toward Iwo Jima. As the Americans moved toward the island, the Imperial Navy made a desperate effort to halt their progress by launching *kaiten* or torpedoes guided by swimmers against 5th Fleet ships. The effort was a dismal failure. When D-Day dawned, all was ready for a swift occupation of the island.

Shortly after 0900, the first assault wave hit the beaches. Within minutes, the Japanese launched a savage mortar attack which caught American forces off guard and pinned them down on the beaches. It was only after the resumption of naval bombardment that Japanese mortars and machine guns were silenced and this proved to be only temporary as Admiral Blandy was no more successful than Navy and Army pilots had been in knocking out enemy defenses. No sooner did American gunfire stop than Japanese fire commenced.

Although the Japanese had made the landings on Iwo Jima difficult and extracted a toll of more than 3000 dead, wounded, or missing in action, by the end of D-Day some 30,000 Americans had been put ashore on Iwo Jima. Many more were to follow on succeeding days. The Japanese, by contrast, were not able to reinforce their garrison on Iwo Jima which numbered approximately 23,000 on 19 February. The Imperial Navy had run its last Tokyo Express in October 1944 off Leyte, forcing General Kuribayashi, commanding officer of the Japanese garrison on Iwo Jima, to resort to new tactics.

Contrary to American assumptions following the first day of battle on Iwo Jima, Kuribayashi did not counterattack. To the contrary, he held his forces in reserve and retreated to previously prepared strongholds further inland and hence somewhat safer from naval bombardment. There the Japanese waited, hoping to lure the Marines into a yard-by-yard contest for the island. Although their numbers were considerably smaller than their enemy's, Japanese forces enjoyed superior defensive positions and were not dependent upon close naval artillery support.

Thanks to support received from 5th Fleet carriers and support craft, American forces moved slowly toward Mount Suribachi, eventually taking this high ground on 23 February in a moment captured and immortalized by an Associated Press photographer. By 25 February, the Japanese had been isolated in the northernmost part of Iwo Jima and Seabees were readying two of the island's airstrips for B-29 landings. It was not, however, until 16 March that Major General Harry Schmidt, USM, announced that Iwo

Jima was secured and even then there were isolated pockets of enemy resistance.

The American victory on Iwo Jima was a costly one. By the time the operation officially ended on 27 March, 25,000 Americans had been injured or killed with the Japanese losing an equal number of men, almost their entire garrison. For both sides, this battle was one of the most costly and savage of the whole war. It boded ill for the upcoming operation in Okinawa which was being planned even as the battle on Iwo Jima dragged on. Okinawa was strategically more important than Iwo Jima. Situated almost midway between Japan and Formosa, Okinawa was to be the base from which the invasion of Japan would be launched sometime later in 1945 or early in 1946. If the Allies failed to secure this island, the occupation of Japan would be set back months, perhaps indefinitely. Thus, no effort was to be spared to take the island but there were many serious obstacles to overcome.

Okinawa, unlike Iwo Jima, was a large island defended by a Japanese garrison numbering in excess of 100,000 men. There were numerous air bases on the island and it was close enough to Japanese fields on Kyushu to permit home based craft to contest an enemy force of occupation. Any large amphibious operation on Okinawa was sure to encounter stiff resistance on land and in the air, not to say anything of the menace of kamikaze attacks launched from Okinawa and Japanese fields. It was no wonder, then, that Allied preparations for an attack on Okinawa were the most elaborate of the Pacific War.

Responsibility for Operation Iceberg, as the invasion of Okinawa had been dubbed, was shared by Mitscher, Spruance, and Turner, who were also responsible for the Iwo Jima campaign, and Lieutenant General Simon Bolivar Buckner, Tenth Army USA. Buckner commanded nearly 300,000 men who were to be landed on Okinawa beginning 1 April 1945. Transporting, supplying, and protecting this massive assault force was an unprecedented venture in the Pacific which taxed even

Left : The 4th Marine Division moving up the beach of Iwo Jima. These men were part of Major General Harry Schmidt's V Amphibious Corps and had already participated in three major and successful amphibious operations in eighteen months.

Left: 40mm Bofors AA guns of the battleship *West Virginia* (BB. 48) are ready for action off Okinawa on L-Day. The *West Virginia* had been extensively rebuilt after suffering damage at Pearl Harbor in December 1941.
Right: The battleship *New Mexico* (BB. 40) bombarding Okinawa in April 1940.
Far right: *LST. 829* during the Okinawa invasion with a landing pontoon lashed to her side.
Left below: The Japanese battleship *Yamato*, accompanied by a destroyer, is under attack north of Okinawa. She is down at the bow and shrouded in smoke after multiple hits.
Bottom: A Japanese escort founders after a bomb hit by North American B-25s of the Air Apache Group. This photograph was taken south of Okinawa on 29 March 1945.

the experience and know-how of senior 5th Fleet commanders.

Over 250 ships were gathered to transport Tenth Army to Okinawa escorted by a joint Anglo-American support group of battleships, cruisers, and aircraft carriers. Prior to D-Day, the carriers conducted numerous missions against enemy bases in Japan in order to diminish aerial interference with the landings. In the process, three carriers were damaged by kamikaze attacks but they were not lost thanks to new firefighting techniques. Aerial and naval bombardment of known enemy strongholds also preceeded the landings but like the situation on Iwo Jima, they were ineffective given the subterranean nature of Japanese defense on Okinawa.

1 April 1945 was D-Day for Operation Iceberg. On that morning the first American forces waded ashore shortly

after 0830 and much to their surprise, they encountered no enemy resistance. By the end of the day over 50,000 men had been put ashore with no casualties except for those resulting from unloading mishaps and two kamikaze attacks on retiring transports. The absence of the enemy on the beaches was a blessing but it was also a bit spooky. No one expected the Japanese to give up Okinawa without a fight. The question was where and when their counterattack would come.

In preparing to defend Okinawa, the Japanese had assembled the most formidable array of force on land and in the air that the Americans had encountered during the Pacific War. Their strategy was to lure American forces away from the beaches into the interior where they had constructed a complex of interconnected cave-like fortifications reminiscent of Tarawa

and Iwo Jima. While American ground units pursued this bait, an all-out effort would be made to destroy the 5th Fleet by suicide missions the likes of which had not yet been experienced in the Pacific.

During the first weeks of the Battle for Okinawa, kamikaze attacks were systematically launched against American and British naval vessels which had sealed off the island. Furthermore, a floating suicide mission employing the *Yamato* and the few operating battle wagons left in the Imperial Navy was dispatched from Japan to Okinawa to finish off those ships which kamikaze pilots failed to sink. Resort to this kind of attack was, in retrospect, a measure of the desperation of the Imperial Government.

Thanks to intelligence provided by American submarines, the *Yamato* and her consorts were tracked from the

Inland Sea to Okinawa. When this group reached Okinawa on 7 April, it was immediately attacked by hundreds of American aircraft. Shortly after 1230, the *Yamato* was hit by a bomb. Ten minutes later two additional bombs and one torpedo found their mark. During the next hour, additional hits were scored causing this giant vessel to list to near 35 degrees. When she went under at about 1420, nearly 2500 men lost their lives.

It was fortunate that the *Yamato* had been spotted before reaching the 5th Fleet. Before departing from Japan for her final voyage, the *Yamato* had been armed with thousands of rounds for her batteries. Although she had only enough fuel and provisions for a one-way trip to Okinawa, given her speed and artillery potential, the *Yamato* could have wrought havoc with the Allied armada before finally

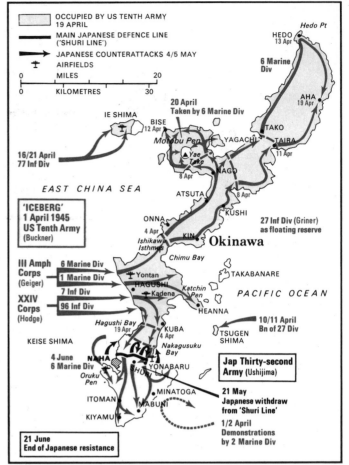

Above left: The heavy cruiser *Chester* (CA. 27) patrols the waters off Okinawa in May 1945.
Left: The destroyer *Longshaw* (DD. 559), three minutes after the forward magazine blew up, following hits by Japanese artillery off Okinawa on 18 May 1945. The ship sank later that day.

succumbing. With the sinking of the *Yamato*, the Imperial Japanese Navy had only one battleship left.

Although their desperate effort to disrupt the Allied landings on Okinawa failed, the Japanese continued to attack American ships. Kamikaze attacks were a daily feature of the Battle for Okinawa. Worse still, these attacks were no longer solo sorties but, rather, massed raids or *Kikusai* (Chrysanthemum raids). Such raids were far more dangerous than individual attacks considering the fact that dozens and sometimes hundreds of aircraft were used in one raid. It was difficult if not impossible to protect all ships against attacks of this kind. Consequently, many Allied vessels were damaged or destroyed.

Between April and June 1945, 3000 kamikaze raids were launched against Allied naval forces off Okinawa. In addition, hundreds of conventional attacks were carried out by Japanese pilots flying from the home islands. By the time the Battle for Okinawa ended. Thirty-six Allied ships had been sunk and 400 others had been hit and damaged; many were beyond repair.

Right top : LSMR (Landing Ships, Medium-Rocket) begin to bombard Okinawa before the invasion.
Right below : The confusion of Okinawa beach, with ships offshore and fuel drums dumped from landing craft.

If Allied naval forces encountered stiff enemy resistance off Okinawa, American ground forces faced an even more hellish situation on the island. As had been the case on Iwo Jima, Japanese defense forces on Okinawa had prepared elaborate subterranean hide-outs and strong-points from which they were prepared to resist their enemies every step of the way. Hardly a yard of ground was taken without loss of life or limb and when the Japanese retreated, it was generally to yet another underground position from which to continue their resistance.

The Battle for Okinawa did not come to an end until 22 June 1945 by which time 49,000 Americans had been wounded or killed. In their defense of Okinawa, the Japanese lost over 100,000 men, a staggering

Below : Men, who had been blown overboard and injured in fire off Okinawa on 9 April 1945, are returned to the escort carrier *Chenango* (CVE. 28) from the destroyer *Guest* (DD. 472).

Above: Admirals Nimitz and Spruance (in sun helmet) visit the front in Okinawa.

number. Except for the Battle for Guadalcanal, the Battle for Okinawa was the longest siege of the Pacific War and certainly the most costly. Of equal importance was the psychological impact of this bloodletting. If the Japanese were willing to sacrifice 100,000 men in the defense of Okinawa, how many would die on both sides when Allied forces invaded Japan proper?

By the time Okinawa was secured, the war in Europe was over and preparations were underway for a final assault on Japan sometime in 1946. Despite the destruction of Japan's Navy and merchant fleet, not to say anything of the decimation of factories and industrial facilities in the large urban centers, Japanese leaders seemed unwilling to surrender. Even the establishment of a naval blockade and the escalation of strategic bombing seemed to have scant effect on the Tokyo government which appeared to be husbanding its resources for the final battle.

In planning for an invasion of Japan, Allied leaders were often preoccupied by the heavy losses that would have to be borne before the Japanese were finally subdued. This concern was voiced as early as the Yalta Conference in February 1945 in an effort to secure a pledge of Soviet participation in the invasion of Japan. From the point of view of the Joint Chiefs of Staff, a Russian commitment to enter the war was not merely desirable, it was a necessity. This position was reinforced by news of the Battle for Iwo Jima which was being fought even as Churchill, Roosevelt and Stalin were meeting at Yalta.

Allied strategists estimated that if the Japanese did not capitulate before the invasion of Japan proper, the occupation of that country might cost as much as one million casualties. Given this nightmare, Roosevelt had little choice but to make concessions to the Soviets to secure their aid. Stalin realized this and struck a hard bargain with the President before he agreed to Russian participation in the final campaign of the Pacific War.

Despite the pledge of Soviet intervention, Anglo-American military leaders were still concerned about achieving a final victory at minimal cost. Given the fact that Churchill and Roosevelt had committed the Allies to the idea of an unconditional surrender without precondition it was not likely that Japanese 'peace-feelers' would come to much nor did it appear likely that there was a viable alternative to the invasion and occupation of Japan, at least for the moment.

After the conclusion of the Battle for Okinawa Nimitz directed Halsey to attack designated targets in Japan in preparation for the final assault. Beginning on 10 July and continuing for weeks thereafter, Allied carrier and land-based planes launched an unprecedented air blitz on Japan supplemented by naval artillery barrages launched from the battleships *Indiana, Iowa, Massachusetts, Missouri, South Dakota* and *Wisconsin*. By the beginning of August these attacks had virtually demolished the Imperial Navy and destroyed much of what was left of Japan's industrial capacity.

As Halsey was carrying out Nimitz's orders, a singular event altered the course of history and the war – President Truman was informed that the Atomic Bomb was ready for use against the enemy. After almost three years of top-secret research, the Allies now seemed possessed of their 'ultimate weapon.' The availability of the A-bomb injected a new element in the discussion of how to obtain the final victory over Japan.

In retrospect, it seems clear that it was inevitable, given the situation at the time, that the Atomic Bomb would be employed against Japan. As Churchill so eloquently pointed out after the war, to Allied leaders this new weapon seemed a 'miracle of deliverance' which would bring the war to an end and 'avoid indefinite butchery' Truman and his advisors shared these sentiments and so it was that the decision was made to use the weapon against the enemy despite the protests of some who had worked on Project Manhattan.

Above left : Anti-aircraft lookouts and talker on a battleship off Okinawa.
Above : A LSM (Landing Ship, Medium) alongside a warship with supplies for Okinawa.

On 6 August 1945 the first atomic weapon to be used in warfare was dropped on the city of Hiroshima, leveling the city and killing over 80,000 people. Three days later, a second Atomic Bomb was dropped on Nagasaki with similarly devastating results. On 10 August the Imperial Japanese Government called for a cease-fire and indicated its willingness to end the war if the Allies promised that the Imperial institution would be preserved in postwar Japan. On 11 August Allied leaders replied that the war would come to an end only if the Japanese accepted the terms of surrender that had been developed at Potsdam and announced in July 1945. There would be no promises in advance concerning Imperial rights.

On 15 August Emperor Hirohito publicly announced Japan's acceptance of an unconditional surrender.

Above right : After being crashed by a kamikaze plane the *Butler* (DMS. 29) is aided by the fleet Tug *Ute* (ATF. 76), as seen from the *West Virginia* (BB. 48), off Okinawa in May 1945.
Right : US cruiser fires her guns at Okinawa.

Above : The atomic bomb explodes at Nagasaki on 9 August 1945. This photo was taken from the plane that dropped the bomb.
Right : The Hiroshima bomb fell about one mile from this area, but the devastation was still total.

Right : Rear Admiral Jesse Oldendorf during the Okinawa operations in August 1945.
Below : The battleship *Tennessee* (BB. 43) in Buckner Bay, Okinawa, 1945. She had been completely rebuilt after Pearl Harbor, but did not return to active duty until 1944.

The following day, Japanese forces were ordered to lay down their arms and cease hostile actions. Allied forces received similar instructions on 15 and 16 August.

On 2 September 1945 Japan formally surrendered in a ceremony held on board the USS *Missouri* anchored in Tokyo Bay. On that historic day, Admirals Nimitz and Halsey joined General MacArthur and other Allied military leaders in accepting Japan's surrender. It was fitting that the *Missouri* was chosen as the site of the formal end of the Pacific War for without the many brave and valiant efforts of the sailors and Marines of the United States Navy, it is doubtful that the Japanese would ever have been defeated.

INDEX

SHIPS

ACKNOWLEDGMENTS

The author wishes to thank Richard Natkiel of *The Economist* for supplying the maps, Charles Haberlein for supplying many of the photographs and David Eldred who designed this book. His special thanks go to Antony Preston who provided some technical assistance for the captions.

The author would also like to thank the United States Navy, which provided all the photographs for this book except for the following:

National Archives: 12, 13 (bottom), 16/17, 26/27, 30/31, 32/33 (top and center), 37 (both), 39 (bottom), 42/43, 46/47, 48 (both), 49 (bottom), 50 (top), 51 (top), 52/53 (all 3), 54/55 (all 5), 56 (center left), 56/57, 57 (center right), 58/59 (all 3), 60 (all 3), 62 (top), 63 (top 2), 64/65 (top and bottom), 66/67, 68/69 (all 4), 71 (both), 72 (top), 73 (top), 74 (top), 75 (all 3), 78/79 (all 3), 80/81 (all 3), 82/83 (all 3), 84/85, 85 (top right), 86, 88/89, 90/91, 92/93, 94/95 (all 4), 96/97 (all 3), 98 (top left), 102/103, 104/105, 106/107 (all 4), 108/109 (all 3), 112, 114/115, 116/117, 117 (top 2), 118/119 (top and bottom), 119 (center), 123 (center and bottom), 124/125, 124 (top left), 125, 126/127, 127 (top left), 128 (all 3), 129 (top), 132 (top), 133 (center), 134/135 (all 5), 136 (bottom), 137 (all 3), 138/139 (all 4), 140 (top 2), 142/143, 144/145 (all 4), 146, 147, 148/149 (all 5), 150/151 (both), 152/153 (all 4), 155 (top), 156/157 (all 3), 158/159 (all 5), 160/161, 162/163 (all 4), 164/165 (all 4), 167 (top 3), 169 (top), 170 (top), 171 (all 3), 173 (top), 174 (bottom 3), 176/177, 179 (top 2 and center right), 182 (top 2), 183 (top 2), 184 (top), 185 (top and bottom), 186/187 (all 4), 189 (both).

US Air Force: 8/9, 9 (top), 38, 43 (top right), 127 (top left), 132/133, 141 (top right), 166/167, 182/183 (bottom), 188 (top left).
Robert Hunt Library: 98 (center), 154, 188 (top right).
Bison Picture Library: 41 (bottom), 43 (top center), 130/131, 140/141.
Orbis: 42 (top), 155 (bottom), 185 (center).
Ted Stone Collection: 22/23 (both).
Defense Dept, Marine Corps: 126 (top).
National Maritime Museum: 24.